HIDDEN HISTORY

of Transportation in

LOS ANGELES

Charles P. Hobbs

THE
History
PRESS

Published by The History Press
Charleston, SC 29403
www.historypress.net

First published 2014

Manufactured in the United States

ISBN 978.1.62619.671.1

Library of Congress Control Number: 2014952247

This book is dedicated to anyone—past, present or future—who has ever had or will have a bright idea to improve transportation in Southern California.

CONTENTS

CONTENTS

ACKNOWLEDGEMENTS

This book could not have been written without the existence and support of several institutions and individuals. Historical societies were an important source of photographs and other information. I would like to acknowledge the Pasadena Museum of History, Burbank Historical Society, Malibu Lagoon Museum, San Pedro Bay Historical Society, Topanga Historical Society and California Historical Society.

I would like to acknowledge the staff of the following public libraries: Los Angeles Public Library, Central Branch; County of Los Angeles Public Library; and public libraries in the cities of Azusa, Burbank, Corona, Fullerton, Glendale, Glendora, Pasadena, Pomona, Ontario, Santa Monica, Simi Valley and Torrance.

Academic libraries (including Special Collections departments) that were invaluable included University of California institutions at Irvine, Los Angeles, San Diego and Santa Barbara; California State University institutions at Fullerton, Los Angeles, Northridge, Pomona and San Diego; University of La Verne; University of Southern California; Pepperdine University; Fullerton College; and Mount San Antonio College.

Libraries specializing in transportation—such as the Dorothy Peyton Gray Transportation Library (Los Angeles County Metropolitan Transportation Authority), the Harmer E. Davis Transportation Library (Institute of Transportation Studies, University of California–Berkeley) and the Transportation Library at Northwestern University—also enabled much of the research that made this book possible.

The law libraries of Los Angeles, Riverside and San Bernardino Counties provided access to California Railroad Commission/California Public Utilities Commission decisions and other legal documents. The Huntington Library; the Library of Congress; the California State Library; the National Archives and Records Administration (in Washington, D.C., and Riverside, California); the Los Angeles City Records Center; and the National Air And Space Museum, Smithsonian Institution, all provided access to important historical records.

Special thanks goes to Matthew Barrett, librarian of the Dorothy Peyton Gray Transportation Library, for making its archives available when I needed them; Christina Rice of the Los Angeles Public Library, for her assistance with the library's photo collection; Michael Holland of the Los Angeles City Records Center; and to Simon Elliott of the UCLA Library Special Collections, for helping me to obtain pictures from the *Los Angeles Times* collection.

I would like to thank the following individuals for granting interviews (in person or by mail, phone or e-mail): Ryan Snyder, Steve Weathers (Bug Line), Bill Forsythe (Forsythe and Associates), Peter Mobley (representing the Carson family), Michael Kadletz (Pink Bus), Mac Barnes (Ground Link), Donald Spivack (LA CRA), Barry Goldwater Jr. (Frank Hendler), Walter Williams (Thomas W. Matthew) and Richard Katz (LA River Freeway).

I would also like to thank the members of Internet Writer's Workshop (IWW) Writing and Nonfiction mailing lists for critiquing my writing and suggesting improvements. The following members of the IWW Nonfiction list stand out as being particularly helpful: G.K. Adams, Diane Diekman, Ellen Dreyer, Tim Elhajj, Paul Fein, June Gallant, Pam Gregory, Mel Jacob, Janaki Lenin, Sarah Corbett Morgan, Cathy Moser, Gary Presley, Loretta Russell and Mona Vanek. However, all of the members on both mailing lists provided much-needed assistance and support.

My commissioning editor, Jerry Roberts, and my cartographer, Tom Wilcockson (Mapcraft.com), also deserve special recognition for all of the ups and downs we went through as we prepared this book. I must also thank Loren P. Meissner, author of *A Brief History of Eastvale* (The History Press, 2013) for letting The History Press know about my book.

Finally, I would like to thank my wife, Angelia, and daughter, Mackenzie, for their support and patience during the seven years required to bring this book to light. All of my family members—my parents, Charles and Marva Hobbs; my in-laws, Hayward and Kizzie; my sisters, Sharon and Susanne; and my wife's siblings, Adriene, Annette and Leroy—helped in one way or another. And above all, thanks to God for perseverance and strength.

INTRODUCTION

Like countless small springs feeding a mighty river, the inspiration for *Hidden History of Transportation in Los Angeles* developed from many small events.

It came partly from growing up in Los Angeles, traveling via the freeways, learning to read maps and listening to radio traffic reports. It also came from my first experience with public transit in the summer of 1984. I commuted three times a week between La Verne and the University of California–Irvine using public transit. The trip, which took about five hours each way, required the use of three Southern California Rapid Transit District (RTD) buses to travel from La Verne to the Orange County line. At Brea, I would transfer to the Orange County Transit District (OCTD) buses to travel farther south to Irvine, with a connection in Santa Ana. Somehow, that onerous and tiring commute led to my lifelong fascination with public transportation.

Later that summer, I rode the bus to downtown Los Angeles. There I noticed the different transit agencies serving the central city—buses of all colors: Santa Monica's "Big Blue Bus," the red-and-white buses of Torrance Transit and Gardena's green-and-yellow buses. Why so many different agencies? Wouldn't it be better to have a single transit agency go everywhere?

By 1987, I had learned that many former independent bus companies had been absorbed into RTD. There were also plans to break apart RTD into several new transit agencies. Intrigued, I sent a letter to RTD inquiring about both the historic bus companies and the future of the agency. A week later, I received a two-part letter.

The first part was a list of former bus companies with names such as "Asbury Rapid Transit," "Blue and White Bus Lines of Watts" and "Pasadena City Lines." These companies became unprofitable in the 1960s and '70s due to increasing labor costs, the proliferation of personal automobiles and other factors. RTD (or its predecessor, Los Angeles Metropolitan Transit Authority), in the interest of providing continued service, acquired the bus companies and integrated their routes into its network.

The second part was a list of RTD bus routes to be taken over by either the City or the County of Los Angeles. These were express and suburban local routes that had become costly for RTD to operate, so the agency was planning to cancel them. The City of Los Angeles was planning to operate ten of these routes under contract to a private bus company. The county also planned to operate six other former RTD routes, again using a private operator under contract.

The words of that letter spoke of the past and future of Southern California public transportation. RTD, which had swallowed whole several smaller bus companies, was now giving routes to several new transit agencies.

In 1987, I also chose a graduate program. Although I had a strong interest in urban planning, I decided to go into library science. As part of a class project, I discovered the RTD Library, which specialized in providing research services to the planning department at the transit agency. During the summer of 1989, I had an internship at the library, working with librarian Dorothy Gray. My project was to organize the library's collection of archival documents; one of my tasks included writing a short history of each bus company acquired by RTD. (Dorothy Gray passed away in late 2001, and the library has been named the Dorothy Peyton Gray Transportation Library in her honor.)

In 1991, I joined the Southern California Transit Advocates, an all-volunteer, grass-roots group supporting improved public transportation. This group was (rightfully) more concerned with current events than with history, so I concentrated my efforts on the deeds and misdeeds of transit agencies and local governments, while keeping my interest in transit history as a hobby.

During long Metrolink commutes in 2006, I would read biographies of all sorts of people ranging from rock musicians to business tycoons. I marveled at the breadth of information the authors found out about their subjects. For example, I did not know the Wilson brothers of the Beach Boys had Swedish ancestry. I thought, "Could I ever write something like this?"

The final impetus for writing this book came in early 2007, as I was experimenting with the Proquest Historical *Los Angeles Times* database at the Los Angeles Public Library. Remembering some of the names of the historical bus operators, I typed in "Motor Transit" and clicked the "Search" button. Proquest returned an amazing number of articles, from which I learned not only about the Motor Transit bus system itself but also about the rich and full life of its founder, O.R. Fuller.

I tried another search on "Blue and White Bus Lines." This search brought up all sorts of information on the Watts-based bus line and Dr. Thomas W. Matthew, the first African American neurosurgeon in the United States. Along with the Watts bus lines, Dr. Matthew had built an empire of organizations, including a bus system in New York, a hospital, apartment buildings and small businesses—all intended to provide black citizens and other marginalized groups a path to self-betterment without resorting to welfare.

A search on "Pink Bus Lines" led to information on Mike Kadletz, who at the young age of eighteen formed a bus company in transit-sparse Orange County to take teenagers to the beach as an alternative to hitchhiking.

I recalled and searched for more stories from Southern California's unique transportation history. Horace Dobbins and his elevated bikeway in Pasadena. Joseph Fawkes's bizarre propeller-powered monorail. The unpopular "Diamond Lane" on the Santa Monica Freeway. A futuristic but financially troubled "people mover" for downtown Los Angeles. A proposal to use the concrete-lined bed of the Los Angeles River as a freeway. Mac Barnes, who stretched the definition of "carpool" by carrying his passengers in a full-size, forty-seven-passenger bus. All seemed to be part of a greater story.

By mid-March 2007, I knew there had to be enough material for a book. Why not chronicle all of these interesting but somewhat forgotten stories in one volume for posterity?

Hidden History of Transportation in Los Angeles brings to life these stories of early transportation operators and events, from the 1900s to the present. Much more than a fact-filled history, it will answer questions like: Who were the people behind these transportation systems? Where did they come from? What motivated them to provide transportation services? And finally, what mark did they leave behind on Southern California's current transportation system?

It is my hope that my book will not only educate and entertain its readers but also inspire the next Fuller, Matthew, Kadletz or Barnes to make their mark on transportation in Southern California.

CHAPTER 1

THE FOOT THAT MOVES THE PEDAL

Horace M. Dobbins's California Cycleway

The foot that moves the pedal is the foot that moves the world." This was supposedly a favorite saying of Horace M. Dobbins, one of Pasadena's most famous citizens. He was best known for the "California Cycleway," an elevated wooden bike path above the streets of Pasadena. His goal was to extend this bikeway to downtown Los Angeles, but he was unable to obtain funding to do so. However, the Cycleway continues to inspire interest in bicycling, particularly as an alternative to the automobile, to this day.

HORACE DOBBINS

Horace M. Dobbins was born on August 29, 1868, the fifth child and youngest son of Richard J. and Caroline Dobbins. The Dobbinses were an old-money family who lived on a one-hundred-acre estate in Cheltenham, near Philadelphia. Richard was a master builder, responsible for many landmarks in Philadelphia, including the Public Ledger Building, the House of Corrections and Memorial Hall, one of several structures for the Centennial Exhibition in 1876.

Richard enrolled young Horace in the Cheltenham Military Academy. But Horace found school difficult, as he preferred to teach himself. This frustrated his father to no end. "Oh Horry, you'll never amount to anything," he would scold.

The Dobbins family moved to Pasadena's milder climate permanently in 1886, as Richard was in poor health. Richard died in early 1893. Horace spent a few years in Portland, Maine, and then in San Diego before settling in Pasadena in 1895.

Dobbins took part in Pasadena's civic life with enthusiasm. He served on the Pasadena Board of Trustees and was president of the Pasadena Board of Health and the Tournament of Roses Board and was active in both the Pasadena and Los Angeles Chambers of Commerce. He also became president of the Pasadena Hospital Association, which built the first successful hospital in Pasadena.

PASADENA AND THE BICYCLE CRAZE

Throughout the 1800s, transportation was limited to walking, horseback, horse-drawn carriages for those who could afford them or, in the larger cities, horse- or mule-drawn streetcars. Although bicycles had existed since the early 1860s, they were the old-fashioned types, with a very high front wheel (for speed). Accidents in which the rider was thrown over the handlebars were common.

By the late 1880s, a new type of bicycle had appeared on the market. Unlike the "high-wheelers," this bicycle featured two equally sized wheels, pneumatic tires and a chain drive between the pedals and the back wheel. This new version was known as the "safety bicycle," as it was much safer to ride than the high-wheeler. It kicked off what became known as the "Bicycle Craze" across the United States, as the bicycle became a mode of transportation almost anyone could afford and use.

More and more people rode bicycles, and bicycle sales increased. Much cheaper to own and maintain than a horse, it provided a new freedom to its riders. This was especially true for women, who reveled in the independence provided by the bicycle. Indeed, many historians credit the Bicycle Craze for partially inspiring the women's liberation movement. Advocate Susan B. Anthony said, "Let me tell you what I think of bicycling. I think it has done more to emancipate women than anything else in the world. I stand and rejoice every time I see a woman on a wheel [bicycle]. It gives a woman a feeling of freedom and self-reliance."

Songs like "Daisy Bell (Bicycle Built for Two)" and "The Bicycle Girl" emanated from music hall and fancy parlor alike. However, sales of pianos and other items fell dramatically as people bought bicycles instead. Bicycling replaced other activities, such as reading, going to the theater or attending church.

Southern California, because of its mild weather, reportedly had more bicycles per person than any other place in the world. Pasadena, in particular, had an active cycling community, several cycling clubs and a high-quality racing track. However, Pasadena lacked good roads for people who used bicycles as a means of transportation rather than as a sport. Cyclists had to contend with dirt roads full of wagon ruts, railroad tracks and horse manure. Riding on the sidewalk was not an option; local mounted police would catch and fine any offenders. Only one road, in very poor condition, joined Pasadena and Los Angeles, making bicycle travel between the two cities difficult.

DOBBINS BUILDS THE CYCLEWAY

Although Horace Dobbins was not an avid cyclist, he was a great dreamer of solutions to problems. One day, while traveling between Pasadena and Los Angeles, he was distressed by the poor road and decided that an improved roadway for bicycles was needed between the two cities.

In August 1897, Dobbins formed the California Cycleway Company. He was the president of the company, and former California governor Henry H. Markham was vice-president.

The company sold stock for twenty dollars per share. These funds, along with money Dobbins had received in an inheritance, were used to purchase a six-mile right-of-way along the Arroyo Seco, a small waterway winding between Pasadena and Los Angeles.

The Cycleway would be an elevated roadway made of Oregon pine, rising from fifteen to fifty feet above the ground. It would be wide enough for two cyclists riding abreast in each direction. The franchise also required that electric lights be placed along the roadway.

It would feature gentle grades, no more than about 3 percent, allowing for nearly effortless pedaling. It would pass through a tunnel under the Elysian Park hills north of central Los Angeles and then end near the Plaza

Merlemount Casino drawing. *From the* Pasadena Daily Evening News.

Pasadena Cycleway construction. *Courtesy of the Archives, Pasadena Museum of History.*

(Olvera Street). From there, cyclists could use one of several paved roads for continued travel.

The Cycleway's most famous feature was to be the Merlemount Casino, located on a hill near the halfway point in Garvanza (now part of Highland Park). This "casino" would not be a gambling facility, but rather a place where cyclists could take a break. The casino would feature shops, restaurants, separate waiting rooms for ladies and gentlemen and a Swiss dairy providing milk for thirsty cyclists.

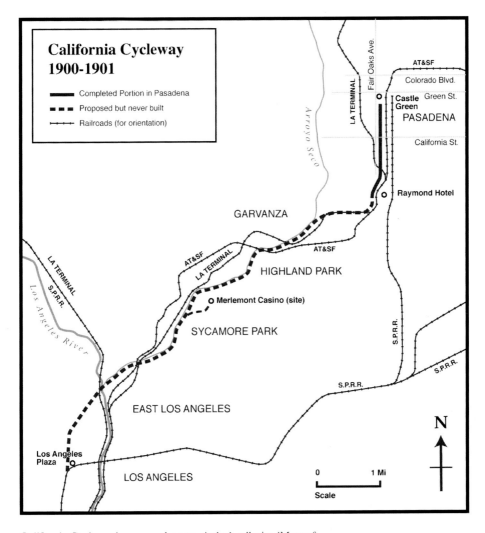

California Cycleway's proposed route. *Author's collection/Mapcraft.*

Work on the Cycleway began on May 6, 1899, with a groundbreaking ceremony at the Casino site. "The earth turns as we turn the earth," declared Dobbins as he dug into the ground.

The magazines of the day wrote of the Cycleway and the Merlemount Casino as if they had already been completed. Writers imagined the completed, lighted Cycleway as a "gleaming serpent" snaking between Pasadena and Los Angeles after dark.

The Cycleway Opens

The Cycleway's first segment, which ran from Dayton Street, south of the Green Hotel, over an alley between Raymond and Fair Oaks Avenues, south to Columbia Street, near the Raymond Hotel, opened for business on January 1, 1900. Although nearly everyone's attention was focused on the eleventh annual Rose Parade, an estimated six hundred cyclists used the Cycleway that day.

At first, everyone enjoyed the Cycleway. Even Dobbins's young daughter, Dorothy, would ride it on her tricycle. The Cycleway franchise also allowed for motorcycles and other motorized vehicles. Dobbins himself traveled on the Cycleway in an early automobile.

On April 16, the Pasadena Board of Trustees elected Dobbins as president, making him mayor of the city.

Cycleway crossing at Opera House. *Courtesy of the Archives, Pasadena Museum of History.*

END OF THE CYCLEWAY

Unfortunately, Dobbins's ambitious project was doomed before the year's end. The Bicycle Craze was winding down, as people abandoned bicycles for other modes of transportation. Henry Huntington and others were expanding their electric trolley networks across Southern California. These streetcars and electric interurban trains would be the dominant mode of transportation for about the next twenty years.

The road improvements that bicyclists demanded also helped usher in the age of the automobile. Horseless carriage pioneers such as Henry Ford had used bicycles as a base for their experimental self-propelled vehicles. By now, the first primitive automobiles had appeared on the roads, and their numbers would only increase in coming years.

Mostly children and athletes now rode bicycles. Prospective Cycleway investors lost interest. Funding to complete the Cycleway beyond Pasadena to Los Angeles, and to build the Casino, never materialized.

The Cycleway Company planned to collect tolls to help finance further expansion. Tolls were ten cents for a one-way trip and fifteen cents for a round trip. Although a tollbooth was placed at the Dayton Street entrance, it was often unmanned, and cyclists rode for free, hurting Dobbins financially.

Work stopped on the Cycleway in October 1900. Dobbins admitted, "Yes, I have concluded that we are a little ahead of the time on this cycleway. Wheelmen have not evidenced enough interest in it, and so we will lie still for a time and use it for an automobile service." Inadvertently, he had forecast the Arroyo Seco Parkway (Pasadena Freeway), to be built nearly forty years later.

Cycleway ticket booth at Green Hotel. *Courtesy of the Archives, Pasadena Museum of History.*

Dobbins riding in an automobile on Cycleway. *Courtesy of the Archives, Pasadena Museum of History.*

He continued, "But those vehicles [automobiles] are not yet common or perfect enough to jump into business. We will preserve our valuable rights of way and then later construct the cycleway on a more substantial plan."

Attitudes toward the Cycleway changed. The citizens of Pasadena voted to acquire land to build Central Park and did not want the elevated structure through it. So, the city acquired the Cycleway structure in the proposed park and demolished it.

THE BRIDGE OF SIGHS

After the Cycleway structure had been removed, Dobbins pondered what to do with his right-of-way. Meanwhile, Henry Huntington's Los Angeles and Pasadena Electric Railway, which became part of the vast Pacific Electric (PE) in 1901, planned a new "short line" between Pasadena and Los Angeles. This new line would cut thirty minutes from the travel time between the two cities. However, the project would require rebuilding the bridge carrying Fair Oaks Avenue over the Santa Fe and Los Angeles Terminal Railroads.

PE planned to replace the existing fifty-two-foot-wide bridge with a new structure of the same width. The City of Pasadena, however, wanted an eighty-two-foot-wide bridge matching the width of Fair Oaks Avenue. Walter Raymond, owner of the nearby Raymond Hotel, also wanted a wider bridge. But the proposed bridge would have taken four feet of Dobbins's property.

Dobbins sued the railway, demanding $15,000 in compensation. PE stopped work on the bridge but continued building the line elsewhere. By October 1902, PE was running short line cars from Los Angeles all the way to the Fair Oaks bridge. From there, passengers had to deboard, walk across the bridge and reboard another trolley for continued travel into Pasadena.

The press labeled the affair the "Bridge of Sighs," after the infamous prison bridge in Venice, Italy. In Pasadena, though, most of the sighing was done by the passengers, who had to put up with the inconvenience of walking across the bridge to change cars.

On November 22, 1902, both parties, weary of the time it was taking for the matter to be heard in the courts, settled. Dobbins received an undisclosed amount in exchange for the necessary land for Pacific Electric to build the wider bridge.

THE PASADENA RAPID TRANSIT COMPANY

Dobbins continued to dream about other uses for his right-of-way. At first, he considered building an elevated road for automobiles, but he decided on an electric interurban railway instead.

On January 1, 1909, Dobbins formed the Pasadena Rapid Transit Company and sold stock for $100 per share. The Pasadena Rapid Transit Company's line would start at an elaborate terminal building near Fifth and Broadway in downtown Los Angeles. It would then run through an underground tunnel to the Los Angeles Plaza before going onward to Pasadena on an elevated structure. The line, featuring two sets of tracks for local and express trains, would carry passengers between the two cities in twelve minutes.

As with the Cycleway, Dobbins was unable to sell enough shares to finance the rail line. A group of Belgians reportedly considered investing but backed out shortly before World War I started.

After the war, Pasadena residents, frustrated with what they thought was poor Pacific Electric service to Los Angeles, decided to revive Dobbins's proposed rail line as a municipally owned service. A measure to issue construction bonds was placed on the April 1919 ballot. While the measure won a majority of votes, it fell short of the two-thirds needed to pass. Project boosters tried again in 1920, but this time, the measure was overwhelmingly voted down. PE, reading the writing on the wall, improved its Los Angeles–Pasadena service.

Dobbins continued his civic activities. In 1909, he became president of the Sixth District Agricultural Association, which managed Agricultural Park in Los Angeles. The park was in poor condition and hosted gambling and other undesirable activities. In 1913, the park was renamed Exposition Park; museums and gardens replaced the racetracks and saloons.

Although he lacked financial and political support to realize them, Dobbins never completely gave up his transportation dreams. He invented and patented a "Lateral Support Monorail" in 1922 and a "Duplex Monorail" in 1929.

In late 1932, Dobbins's relatives in Philadelphia asked him to return to Philadelphia to manage the financially troubled Elks Hotel, which was located on land owned by the Dobbins family. He renamed it the Broadwood Hotel and served as its resident manager for twenty years. Upon retiring, he bought a John Alden yacht and sailed from the East Coast to California via the Panama Canal. He settled in San Pedro, where he traded the boat for an elaborately decorated grand piano. He spent the rest of his life playing the piano and designing yachts but felt lonely because he had outlived so many of his friends.

On September 21, 1962, at the age of ninety-four, Dobbins passed away at Huntington Hospital in Pasadena, the same hospital he helped build in the late 1890s.

EPILOGUE

Although the Cycleway was never completed, it inspired several notable transportation facilities.

In 1938, the State of California built Southern California's first freeway, the Arroyo Seco Parkway, along the banks of the waterway. The parkway opened in 1938 and has carried increasing volumes of traffic over its curving path ever since. Contrary to popular belief, the parkway was not built over the Cycleway's right-of-way but rather on the opposite bank of the Arroyo Seco. (A short portion of the right-of-way exists adjacent to the Metro Gold Line tracks along Fair Oaks in South Pasadena.) Still, Pasadena historians consider Dobbins the "Father of the Freeway" for building one of the first grade-separated transportation facilities in the United States.

The Cycleway north from Raymond Hotel. *Courtesy of the Archives, Pasadena Museum of History.*

Interest in bicycling has increased in the past few decades, as people seek more healthful and environmentally friendly methods of transportation. The County of Los Angeles built a bike path in the concrete-lined bed of the Arroyo Seco in 1983. Unfortunately, several problems plague this path. Rainstorms close the path and leave it strewn with debris for several days afterward. Portions of the path are hidden from street view, posing a security risk. And lastly, a path in the streambed is contrary to the greater environmental goals of returning waterways to their natural states.

Pasadena bicycle advocate Dennis Crowley and Will Dobbins, a grandson of Horace Dobbins, founded a group named California Cycleways in 1996. This organization planned to build an elevated cycleway, similar to the one planned in 1887, between Pasadena and Los Angeles. Construction and maintenance would be financed by tolls. Unfortunately, Crowley's death in 2008 has put a damper on this project. More likely is a new bike path along the Arroyo Seco's banks.

The closest realization of Dobbins's dream happened on June 15, 2003, when the Pasadena Freeway/Arroyo Seco Parkway was closed to motor vehicle traffic but opened to pedestrians and cyclists. Arroyofest, sponsored by the Urban and Environmental Policy Institute of Occidental College, was a joint effort of several environmental, community and bicycle advocacy groups (including Crowley's California Cycleways). As three thousand bicyclists and thousands of pedestrians walked and biked along the eerily silent freeway lanes, residents of South Pasadena and Highland Park heard birds singing instead of traffic noise and noticed the lack of pollution from automobile exhaust. Additionally, residents of the communities along the Arroyo Seco learned of transportation alternatives and connected with their neighbors.

Since October 2010, the City of Los Angeles has supported CicLAvia, a biannual event closing selected city streets to automobiles. More than 100,000 bicyclists, walkers, joggers, skaters and other non-motorized users enjoyed CicLAvia in October 2012.

While the Bicycle Craze may have died down at the turn of the twentieth century, interest in bicycling has never been stronger. Perhaps this rediscovery of the bicycle as a means of transportation will encourage a visionary to build a network of elevated cycleways, as Horace Dobbins attempted in 1900.

CHAPTER 2

"IT'LL PUT THE PACIFIC ELECTRIC RAILROAD IN A MUSEUM!"

Joseph W. Fawkes's Aerial Swallow

FAWKES'S FOLLY

One day in 1907, a small crowd gathered in a Burbank apricot orchard. However, the people did not come to buy fruit. Instead, all attention was focused on a sharply dressed man standing next to an odd-looking object. Upon closer inspection, the strange contraption appeared to be a cigar-shaped vehicle, roughly forty feet long and vaguely resembling a streetcar. It was covered with a shiny metal and featured an airplane-style propeller on one end. The vehicle hung from an overhead steel beam via several wheels and pulleys.

The man, named Joseph Wesley Fawkes, gestured excitedly at the vehicle and shouted to the crowd, "My Aerial Swallow will travel at a top speed of sixty miles per hour. It'll take you from Burbank to Los Angeles in ten minutes. Why, it'll put the Pacific Electric Railroad in a museum!"

The crowd murmured politely, but skepticism hung in the air. Many in Burbank called him "Crazy Fawkes." He had a reputation for being, at best, eccentric. At worst, he was considered standoffish and opposed to anything supported by other people in the city.

Fawkes hopped into the front of the vehicle and started the engine. The propeller spun faster and faster until the Aerial Swallow lurched forward. The crowd murmured in guarded approval.

Fawkes's propeller-powered Aerial Trolley, or Aerial Swallow. *Courtesy, California Historical Society Collection at the University of Southern California. Title Insurance and Trust/C.C. Pierce Photography Collection, CHS-5028.*

The Aerial Swallow traveled about 150 feet. Suddenly, due to engine vibrations, it began to shake itself apart. Fawkes stopped the engine, but his audience, losing interest, began leaving. Mutters of "Crazy Fawkes" and "Fawkes's Folly" filled the air as the crowd dispersed.

JOSEPH WESLEY FAWKES

Joseph Wesley Fawkes was born in Lancaster County, Pennsylvania, in 1861. His father, Joseph Walker Fawkes, was a prolific inventor who developed and patented several agricultural implements, including a steam-powered plow. During the 1860s and 1870s, the Fawkes family moved around Iowa and into Illinois, finally settling in Chicago. The elder Fawkes owned an electrical goods factory in Chicago until 1887, when the business was lost in a fire.

After the fire, the Fawkeses moved to California, settling in Burbank on the land they had purchased in 1884 from David Burbank, the city's namesake. They purchased more land for farms and fruit orchards. But Joseph Wesley Fawkes was no farmer. He spent most of his time writing poetry, painting in oils or traveling around the world. He often expressed views in opposition to other citizens and was frequently found squabbling with most of his family. Most people in Burbank chose to avoid him.

He stood out in other ways as well. While most men wore dungarees and farmers' clothing, Fawkes's store-bought suits were always impeccably neat. He waxed his mustache and went about town in a fancy carriage pulled by two high-stepping horses. As an added touch, a pair of spotted Dalmatian dogs followed the carriage.

Fawkes inherited his father's inventive talents, so he spent much time at the drawing board. In 1901, he patented an electrically illuminated advertising sign. Proceeds from the sales of this device financed his travels and his next invention.

The Aerial Swallow

Although unknown, it's highly possible that one of Fawkes's trips to Europe took him to Wuppertal, Germany, where a suspended monorail, the Schwebebahn, had started operating in 1901. This monorail may have inspired him to build a suspended monorail in Burbank.

Fawkes built a half-mile overhead rail in his orchard, near Lake Street and Olive Avenue, and then constructed his Aerial Trolley Car or Aerial Swallow. On one end was an aircraft propeller, powered by an air-cooled Franklin engine. Aluminum, a comparatively rare metal at the time, encased the forty-foot-long vehicle. The car, which hung from the overhead rail by four wheels, could seat fifty-six passengers. At first, Fawkes planned to add tanks of lighter-than-air gas to the vehicle to improve handling, but he never did so.

Fawkes boasted that the Aerial Swallow would revolutionize transportation. He envisioned extending the monorail along the Los Angeles River to the central city and threatened to build the route "over Mount Hollywood" (in present-day Griffith Park) if the City of Los Angeles refused him permission to build along the riverbank.

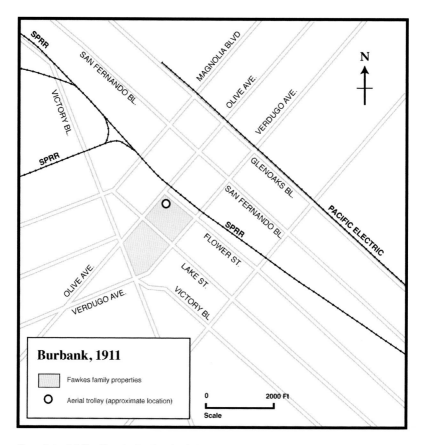

Site of Aerial Swallow in Burbank. *Author's collection/Mapcraft.*

Fawkes's Aerial Swallow. *Courtesy, California Historical Society Collection at the University of Southern California. Title Insurance and Trust/C.C. Pierce Photography Collection, CHS-5013.*

PEOPLE OF BURBANK: NOT INTERESTED

The citizens of Burbank, who were generally put off by Fawkes's antics, were even less impressed by his monorail. Instead, they focused their attention on the transportation system everyone in Southern California wanted a part of: the Pacific Electric "Red Cars."

Although PE had linked Los Angeles and Glendale since 1904, access for Burbank consisted of a trip to Glendale in either a horse-drawn carriage or the "Auto Stage," an early form of bus. Both required travel over bumpy, dusty, unpaved roads. Southern Pacific's passenger trains between Burbank and Los Angeles were also available.

The citizens of Burbank knew that a PE line meant more than transportation; it would be a catalyst for the development, growth and future prosperity of their city. And unlike the Aerial Swallow, the PE was known as a dependable and proven transportation system.

At first, PE refused to extend its rails to Burbank, citing its low population of five hundred. Under continued pressure from the city, PE relented and agreed to build a spur track between Glendale and Burbank—as long as Burbank provided $48,000 before the end of 1910. The citizens immediately began raising funds, while farmers along the proposed route set aside parts of their lands for the rail right-of-way. A number of Burbank landowners lived as far away as San Diego and Riverside, then about one day's journey over primitive roads. Volunteers made the long trip from Burbank to ask these distant landowners to contribute a few thousand dollars each before the end of the year.

Money in hand, PE began work on the track. On September 6, 1911, the first Red Cars made their forty-five-minute run from Los Angeles to Burbank.

FAWKES'S FABULOUS FOURTH

Undeterred by the lack of public support, Fawkes continued to improve his monorail. He obtained a patent in 1911 and formed the Aerial Trolley Car Company. He sold shares in the company for $100; the funds would build not only the monorail but also residences, warehouses, farms and even amusement parks along the route.

Visitors take a ride on the Aerial Swallow. *Courtesy, California Historical Society Collection at the University of Southern California. Title Insurance and Trust/C.C. Pierce Photography Collection, CHS-5015.*

In 1912, he felt that the Aerial Swallow was ready for a public exhibition. On July 4, Fawkes held an extravagant outdoor picnic at his orchard. There was food, music and, after dark, fireworks. But the center attraction was the monorail. Guests clambered aboard the vehicle from a makeshift platform of planks and sawhorses. A sharp whistle blew, and the car moved along the short test track.

The top speed was about three miles per hour, not only slower than the Red Car but also slower than walking. Fawkes's guests must have asked themselves whether the Aerial Swallow would ever be capable of whisking passengers to Los Angeles in ten minutes, as Fawkes had promised.

Since the test vehicle had a propeller on only one end, it had to be pushed back by hand to the starting point to provide multiple trips. The propeller produced an air current, making the open-sided car drafty and uncomfortable.

Although Fawkes's guests enjoyed the food and fireworks, few were impressed enough to invest in the Aerial Trolley Car Company. The event received little coverage in the press; the *Los Angeles Times* printed only a short paragraph, while the *Burbank Review* ignored it entirely.

In spite of Burbank's tepid response, Fawkes continued to promote the Aerial Swallow. He used it to move baskets of apricots across his orchard. Once in a while, a curious person would come to the orchard and take a ride.

SANTA MONICA

Fawkes offered to build an Aerial Trolley in the city of Santa Monica in November 1911. The Santa Monica route would operate along Fremont Street (now Pico Boulevard) from the beach to the city's eastern border, with a future extension eastward to downtown Los Angeles. Six tracks would be provided, allowing for local and express services. Again, the inventor promised phenomenal speeds and travel times: 120 miles per hour and ten minutes to Los Angeles.

In April 1912, he applied to the City of Santa Monica for a franchise. Fares would be five cents for a trip within Santa Monica and ten cents to Los Angeles. A short film of the Aerial Swallow running on its test track played in a local theater, generating interest in the monorail.

However, businesses and property owners on Fremont Street expressed their opposition to the Aerial Trolley, leading the city council to reconsider awarding the franchise. Fawkes remarked, "I was amazed at the stand taken by council in reconsidering the franchise advertisement, but I can see where they stood with all the opposition which developed. I think they were needlessly alarmed." He continued to insist that the Aerial Trolley would be a practical transportation system and not merely an "amusement feature."

On June 4, the city council voted to grant Fawkes the franchise. He invited the citizens of Santa Monica to visit his property in Burbank and see the monorail on its test track. However, the Fremont Street protesters—now joined by the chamber of commerce, the board of trade and the school board—continued to state their opposition to the project. The city council postponed awarding the franchise on June 6.

Support for the monorail continued to grow, with people in Santa Monica's Fairview Heights neighborhood especially enthusiastic. Several Santa Monicans visited the test track in Burbank, and nearly four hundred people signed a petition in favor of the project. The *Evening Outlook* newspaper, which held a strong pro–Aerial Trolley position, complained that it was receiving too many letters in favor of Fawkes.

Finally, on July 2, the city council approved the franchise. But to everyone's astonishment, Fawkes decided not to build the monorail. He complained that the franchise did not prohibit the building of a competing surface trolley along the same route. He also objected to the franchise requirement to carry public officials for free. So, Fawkes slunk back to Burbank, to the relief of the opposition.

Meanwhile, PE had improved several of its routes serving Santa Monica, and the citizens of Santa Monica, as did their counterparts in Burbank, looked to the Red Cars as their primary means of transportation.

"CONSOLIDATION JOE"

Fawkes also found himself at odds with Burbankians over whether Burbank should be a separate incorporated city or annex itself to the city of Los Angeles. In 1908, Los Angeles had started building a 223-mile-long aqueduct to bring water from the far-off Owens Valley to a fast-developing, thirsty Southern California. Although Burbank had its own water wells, Fawkes thought that the city would be better off if it could access water from the aqueduct. Because the legislation authorizing construction of the aqueduct prohibited Los Angeles from selling or giving away water to other cities, if Burbank or any other city wanted aqueduct water, its only choice was to be annexed to Los Angeles.

Despite Fawkes's best efforts, the citizens of Burbank voted overwhelmingly to incorporate as an independent city on July 8, 1911. On November 5, 1913, the first cascades of Owens Valley water arrived in Los Angeles. Most of the small towns in the San Fernando Valley became a part of Los Angeles about two years later. As public interest in his Aerial Swallow waned, Fawkes again pushed for Burbank to be consolidated with Los Angeles.

After an unsuccessful court battle with the city in early 1920 over water bonds, Fawkes again agitated for annexation. He presented a petition with 432 signatures to the city clerk, placing the annexation question on the November ballot. Again, the people voted against annexation. Fawkes, making accusations of ballot box stuffing and other irregularities, petitioned for a special election. A district court of appeal denied the request in 1922, the same year Fawkes unsuccessfully ran for county supervisor.

In preparation for the June 1925 election, Fawkes held several pro-annexation meetings. A meeting held at his home was delayed by an electrical outage. Again, the pro-annexation measure failed to receive sufficient votes. Upon the defeat of the measure, the anti-annexationists held a big party. They lit a bonfire, hung Fawkes in effigy and buried him in a mock grave. "Here lies the body of Consolidation Joe," read the fake headstone.

EPILOGUE

Joseph Wesley Fawkes passed away on June 27, 1928, leaving little more than the Aerial Swallow, which rusted in place until it was hauled away as scrap in 1947. Meanwhile, the Pacific Electric's service to Burbank continued until 1956, when buses replaced the interurban trains. Borrmann Steel relocated from Oakland to the site of the monorail in the 1960s and operates (as the Borrmann Metal Center) to this day.

Although the Aerial Trolley Car was not a success, it remains part of the lore of Burbank. Interest in monorails as viable public transportation has continued; however, no one has yet proposed a propeller-driven monorail based on Joseph Wesley Fawkes's design.

CHAPTER 3

FROM NICKEL-SEEKERS TO SMART SHUTTLES

The Jitney in Southern California

It is the summer of 1915. A man stands at a Los Angeles Railway stop on Main Street in downtown Los Angeles, waiting to board a "Yellow Car." Several overcrowded streetcars have already passed by. Suddenly, from the Model Ts and other automobiles going past, one veers toward the stop and halts.

Attached to the front of the car is a sign: "Jitney Bus. Main and 58ᵗʰ Street. 5 Cents." The auto is filled with riders, and four people are standing on the running boards, holding on for dear life. The driver calls out to the man: "Need a ride?"

The man thinks for a moment. The offer seems risky. Getting into an automobile full of strangers? Then another overcrowded streetcar passes by. Anxious to go home, the man steps toward the overloaded Ford, nickel in hand.

THE JITNEY ARRIVES IN LOS ANGELES

The first automobiles appeared in Los Angeles as early as 1897. Until the advent of the Ford Model T and other mass-produced vehicles, automobiles were regarded as curiosities and, later, as "rich man's toys." The average person would probably never ride in an automobile other than a taxi. Most people either walked or used rail transit, such as Henry Huntington's Los Angeles Railway and the Pacific Electric, controlled by the Southern Pacific Railroad. PE and LARY had a near monopoly on transportation in Los

Angeles. Streetcars were often crowded and sometimes ran late. Newspaper articles painted the streetcar companies as an unresponsive "Trolley Trust," maximizing profits over passenger convenience by allowing overcrowding and ignoring passenger complaints.

The first jitney drivers, such as L.P. Draper of Los Angeles and A.H. Kirkendall of Long Beach, began to offer rides to people waiting at streetcar stops in 1914. Drivers and streetcars charged the same fare: a nickel. At first, people called the vehicles "five cent autos." "Jitney" was common slang for a nickel coin, and eventually, the automobiles themselves were called "jitneys."

Within a year, the jitney phenomenon had spread across most of the United States. Starting a jitney service in most cities was laughably easy. All anyone needed was an automobile and driver's license (as well as, in some cities, a professional chauffeur's license).

There were both full-time and part-time jitney drivers. Often, someone driving to work would pick up and drop off people along the way, charging a fare. "Moonlighting" taxi drivers or private chauffeurs used their cars as jitneys without their employers' knowledge.

As more people discovered that jitney driving was a source of "easy money," more and more full-time jitney drivers appeared on the streets. It was a gold rush. Used Ford Model Ts and similar automobiles, in good or not-so-good condition, flew off the lots. These vehicles were not designed for continuous use, so the drivers switched to larger, heavier touring cars or custom-built bus bodies on truck chassis.

Some jitney drivers liked to be called "jitneurs," a French-sounding combination of "jitney" and "chauffeur." Less complimentary names included "auto-sniper" and "nickel-seeker."

EVERYONE LOVES A JITNEY RIDE

Because the vehicle made fewer stops along the way, jitney riders enjoyed faster service. Jitneys boarded and let off passengers at the curb rather than in the middle of the street, as streetcars did. Sometimes, jitney drivers deviated from their route to drop passengers off closer to their destination, an impossibility for a streetcar. The rubber-tired automobiles also offered a smoother ride than the steel wheels and jointed rails of the streetcar lines. And jitneys just seemed more fun to ride.

We rave like mad if we have to stand up in a street car for four blocks—

But we will ride ten deep in a four-passenger jitney and compliment the driver on his service.

"What a queer lot we are anyway!" *Courtesy of the Jay N. "Ding" Darling Wildlife Society.*

Newspapers and magazines were filled with poems and stories about jitneys. Novelty songs such as "Gasoline Gus and His Jitney Bus," "Jitney Jim" and "I Didn't Raise My Ford to Be a Jitney" became popular.

Many people chose the jitney as a way of striking back at the streetcar companies' overcrowded cars, inconvenient service and unresponsive management. And during the tough times of the mid-1910s, jitneys provided a source of income to the men (and occasionally women) behind the wheel. Government regulations were almost nonexistent, so drivers could work as much or as little as they wanted.

THE JITNEY BECOMES A MENACE

Although many people loved jitneys, this new mode of transportation caused serious problems on the streets of Los Angeles.

Competition for fares caused drivers to operate without regard for the safety of either their passengers or other people on the street. Drivers raced one another to streetcar stops, running over pedestrians or colliding with other vehicles. Los Angeles's vehicle accident rate rose by a startling 60 percent.

Jitneys were sometimes dangerously overloaded. The same passengers who had bitterly complained about having to stand in a streetcar had no problem piling into crowded jitneys, sitting on laps or hanging on to the outside of the car. Drivers defended overloading: the more people they could carry, the more money they made.

Drivers skimped on maintenance. Cars with bald tires, bad brakes and other mechanical problems created additional safety hazards. Most jitney drivers lacked insurance, making it difficult or impossible for persons injured in an accident to recover damages. Police checks frequently turned up drivers who were unlicensed, underage, illiterate or otherwise unqualified.

Jitneys operated according to the whims of their drivers rather than the needs of their riders. If a driver felt he was not making enough money along a given route, he might simply turn around and head back downtown for more passengers, stranding passengers on the outer portion of the route. The more unscrupulous drivers would falsely state that the car had broken down and would need to return downtown, only to order their current load of passengers out of the vehicle.

Drivers gouged riders on fares. A streetcar strike might send the usual nickel fare soaring to as high as a dollar. Bad weather might be an excuse to boost fares or to not drive at all, leaving people without transportation.

Antisocial behavior was common among jitney drivers. Fistfights broke out among drivers competing for fares. Racial discrimination was prevalent; jitney drivers often refused to carry black citizens and other minorities.

The overcrowded jitneys were an ideal place for pickpockets to ply their trade. Some drivers were criminals who supplemented their income by robbing passengers. The close confines of the jitneys attracted gropers and sexual harassers. Women were warned not to use the jitneys unaccompanied, especially at night. And there were the fake jitneys, used to attract passengers for criminal purposes. An attitude of "anything goes in the jitneys" prevailed, giving them a bad reputation.

NOT ENOUGH NICKELS FOR BOTH OF US

At first, the streetcar companies ignored the jitneys. Streetcar company executives thought that drivers would lose interest as repair costs and depreciation ate into their profits. But as the number of jitneys increased and more people chose them over the streetcar, the streetcar companies lost money.

Jitneys concentrated on serving the busier portion of the streetcar routes near downtown, where the streetcar companies made their profit, enabling them to provide service to the less lucrative outer portion of the routes. As profits fell, the companies reduced service, laid off employees and postponed extending streetcar lines. The Los Angeles Railway considered replacing its popular five-cent flat fare with a distance-based fare system, hoping to recover the costs of serving the outlying parts of its service area.

Paul Shoup, president of Pacific Electric, declared, "There are not enough nickels used for transportation…to support the two classes of transportation."

Hoping to sway public opinion, Pacific Electric and Los Angeles Railway emphasized the public service that their franchises required. Streetcar companies paid taxes; jitney drivers did not. Streetcar companies helped maintain the streets; jitneys just caused them to need repaving more quickly. Streetcar companies carried policemen and firemen for free and offered reduced fares for schoolchildren. Jitneys charged everyone the same price and often overcharged passengers.

The *Los Angeles Times* took a strident anti-jitney position, railing against the "evil of the jitney bus" in its editorials, and dutifully reported nearly every jitney accident. Businesses relying on streetcars to bring in customers sided with the rail operators. So did real estate developers, who truly owed much of their existence to the streetcar's ability to make land accessible for development. Streetcar company management and employee unions put aside their differences and joined forces against the jitney.

By April 1917, the United States had entered World War I. The War Industries Board, encouraged by the streetcar companies, looked askance at jitney drivers duplicating streetcar service and decided they could be doing more essential work—or enlisting in the military.

Although an earlier statewide effort to regulate jitneys had failed, Los Angeles city officials placed Proposition 4 on the June 1917 ballot. The measure, if passed, would ban jitneys from the busiest streets in downtown Los Angeles. It would also require drivers to post an $11,000 bond, choose and adhere to a specified route and operate for a minimum number of hours each day.

The streetcar companies offered free rides to voters and promised raises to their employees. Not surprisingly, the proposition won.

The final blow for jitney operations in central Los Angeles came in 1918, when the city passed an ordinance forbidding jitneys from operating on any street with a streetcar route. Some jitney drivers set up shop in other parts of the city, such as San Pedro, where oversight was much less rigorous. Others found a new home in jitney-friendly suburbs such as Santa Monica or Long Beach; these jitney operations eventually became Santa Monica Municipal Bus Lines and Long Beach Transit. The new, fast-growing "auto stage" (intercity bus) industry also attracted many former jitney drivers.

Jitneys temporarily appeared in Los Angeles during transit labor disputes in 1935 and 1946.

JITNEYS OF THE 1970S: LA FRANCE AND YELLOW CAB

The streetcars made their final run in 1963 and were replaced by diesel buses. The publicly owned Southern California Rapid Transit District (RTD) replaced several privately owned transit companies and extended routes to previously unserved areas.

But Los Angeles city officials, including Mayor Tom Bradley, were looking for other ways to improve transit. They thought that legalized jitneys could supplement bus service along busy streets such as Wilshire Boulevard or provide service in poorly served outlying areas.

RTD reacted to the city's proposal in much the same way the streetcar companies did to the "nickel autos" of the mid-1910s. Jitneys would congest streets, "skim the cream off our best paying lines" and "draw patronage from the guts of our service," protested RTD officials. In spite of the transit agency's complaints, the city council voted to allow two jitney experiments.

In April 1974, Fred La France, an airline operations manager, received a permit to start a jitney route between Marina Del Rey and Venice. His La France Transportation System charged twenty-five cents for a ride in a nineteen-passenger van. La France planned to expand service to Santa Monica, Westchester and Mid-City Los Angeles, but he faced opposition from RTD, Santa Monica Municipal Bus Lines and other transportation companies. Financial difficulties forced him to double his fare to fifty cents.

Yellow Cab started a jitney service on August 5. Green-colored sedans (to distinguish them from regular cabs) ran along fixed routes on Wilshire and Sunset Boulevards. The fare was one dollar—more expensive than RTD's twenty-five cents but cheaper than a taxi. The company planned to add four more routes and replace the cabs with fifteen-passenger vans if the service was successful.

When RTD drivers went on strike on August 12, people needing transportation filled the jitneys. But after the strike ended on October 18, the jitneys lost most of their passengers to RTD's twenty-five-cent fare. Both the Yellow Cab and La France operations ceased in November.

Even though La France and Yellow Cab were unsuccessful, advocates hoped that jitneys would return to the streets of Southern California. Activist groups in East Los Angeles, right-leaning think tanks such as the Reason Foundation and the Cato Institute and United States senator S.I. Hayakawa all expressed support for jitneys.

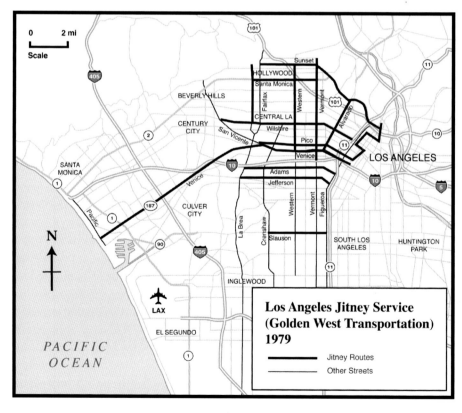

Los Angeles Jitney Service map, 1979. *Author's collection/Mapcraft.*

JACK'S JITNEYS

When a strike once again idled RTD buses in September 1979, Jack Ohan, president of Goldenwest Transportation, applied for and received a temporary permit from the City of Los Angeles to run jitneys along several major streets for the duration of the strike.

Twenty minivans, each hurriedly stenciled with "L.A. Jitney Service," operated along ten routes, mostly in central and western Los Angeles. A few routes served southwestern Los Angeles, and one route replaced RTD's downtown minibus shuttle.

Stranded bus riders crammed into the sixteen-passenger minivans. The small vehicles were not realistic replacements for RTD's usual forty-foot buses; overcrowding and pass-ups were the order of the day. Illegal jitneys, which appeared during the strike, provided unwelcome competition.

Fortunately, the strike only lasted for six days. Once the buses returned, Ohan's minivans disappeared from the streets. Although his jitney experiment cost him about $18,000, Ohan was happy to have served so many people during a time of need.

EXPRESS TRANSIT DISTRICT AND MAXI-TAXI

In 1982, two new companies were formed to run jitneys in Southern California. Francisco, Manuel and Aurelio Medinilla, three brothers from Mexico, founded the Express Transit District (ETD). Another company, Maxi-Taxi, was started by three Russian immigrants. (Jitneys were, and still are, common in big cities in Mexico, Russia and other countries.)

Both companies proposed routes operating between downtown and west Los Angeles, with stops in Santa Monica, Culver City and Beverly Hills. A few routes would operate in South Los Angeles and the San Fernando Valley. Since the routes would cross city borders, both companies required certificates from the California Public Utilities Commission (CPUC). RTD, as well as the Santa Monica and Culver City municipal bus systems, objected fiercely to the upstart companies sharing their routes and bus stops. But in July 1982, CPUC gave its authorization, and soon ETD jitneys were on the roads.

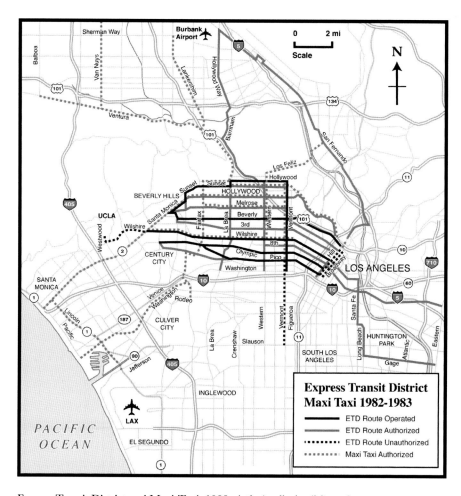

Express Transit District and Maxi-Taxi, 1983. *Author's collection/Mapcraft.*

Although ETD was granted authority for fourteen routes, only six routes operated. Maxi-Taxi, which was authorized to run on an additional thirteen routes, went out of business before it ever provided service.

ETD's ridership peaked at 6,500 daily boardings. Its fifteen-passenger vans were especially popular with Hispanics because of the large number of Spanish-speaking ETD drivers. ETD also provided speedier and friendlier service than the large RTD buses.

However, RTD had an advantage over the private company. In 1980, Los Angeles County voters passed Proposition A, a half-cent sales tax increase to fund a rail system and other transit projects. One provision of Proposition

A held RTD bus fares at fifty cents for three years. But opposition to the proposition kept the money tied up in court battles for more than two years. Finally, in July 1982, RTD was able to get the funds and lower its fares.

ETD originally planned to charge seventy-five cents per ride. But the lowered RTD fares forced ETD to charge fifty cents as well. (RTD's fifty-cent fare was one of the reasons Maxi-Taxi never started operating.) While ETD struggled with the reduced revenue brought on by the lower fare, RTD continued to complain bitterly about ETD vehicles blocking buses at bus stops and "poaching" its passengers.

Eventually, ETD's lack of income took its toll. In April 1983, CPUC, responding to reports of poor maintenance, suspended ETD's certificate. In addition, the Los Angeles County district attorney opened an investigation into ETD for alleged investment fraud. Allegedly, investors who purchased ETD vans received fake bills of sale. In some cases, the same vehicle was "sold" four or five times. The California Department of Labor expressed concern about ETD's bus leasing program. Drivers had to "rent" their vehicles from the company and apply fares toward the rental fee, resulting in them being paid below minimum wage. Other employees, such as mechanics, were never paid.

The Medinillas allegedly returned to Mexico, and ETD went out of business.

SMART SHUTTLE: HIGH-TECH JITNEYS FOR THE 1990s AND BEYOND?

Transportation planners have struggled to design a transit system combining the efficiency of the fixed-route bus and the flexibility of the automobile or taxi. Such a system would be so popular it would pay for itself entirely from the farebox—no government subsidy needed.

This was the promise of Smart Shuttle, an idea originating with the UCLA Urban Innovations Group and later adopted by the Southern California Association of Governments. Small buses would run along major streets. Using high-tech methods such as Global Positioning Systems (GPS) and Automatic Vehicle Location (AVL), dispatchers would be aware of the location of each vehicle at all times. If a passenger needed to be picked up from an off-route location, the dispatcher could easily call the nearest vehicle and have its driver go off route to pick up the passenger and then return

Smart Shuttle vans in San Fernando Valley. *Author's collection.*

to the route. Although the service would operate like a taxi, fares would be closer to fixed-route bus fares.

In 1997, the Metropolitan Transportation Agency (MTA) and the Los Angeles Department of Transportation (LADOT) implemented a pilot Smart Shuttle program in three areas of Los Angeles: Koreatown, South Central and the San Fernando Valley. Although MTA provided $10 million in startup funds, Smart Shuttle was expected to be entirely self-supporting within two years.

Unfortunately, Smart Shuttle did not live up to expectations. In an attempt to match service levels to actual use, Smart Shuttle staff constantly modified routes, service areas and hours and days of operation. Riders were confused as to when the service would be available and whether or not route deviations would be allowed.

On the Koreatown and San Fernando Valley routes, Smart Shuttles simply operated like the jitneys of the 1910s, duplicating MTA bus service and carrying most of the same passengers.

Smart Shuttle never came close to supporting itself entirely from fares. MTA provided an extra $2.3 million in 1999 to keep the shuttles rolling for a little while longer. During the MTA bus strike in 2000, Smart Shuttle enjoyed increased ridership, as desperate passengers crowded onto the vehicles. After a contentious debate between MTA and LADOT as to which would be responsible for the service, all funding was abruptly cut, and Smart Shuttle stopped running in late 2001.

EPILOGUE

It is the summer of 2025. A man stands at a bus stop on Main Street in downtown Los Angeles. A continuous stream of automobiles and small vans passes by. He taps the screen of his smartphone a few times. Suddenly, a small van pulls over to the curb. The man exchanges a few pleasantries with the driver and then gets in the van. No money changes hands; payment has been handled electronically. The van zooms away.

Is this the future of public transportation in Los Angeles? Jitney advocates would like to think so. Groups concerned about those without transportation point to both the increased mobility and employment opportunities jitneys might provide. Libertarians and others ideologically opposed to tax subsidies for public transit favor replacing tax-subsidized bus and rail systems with unsubsidized jitneys.

Technology such as Internet-enabled cellphones can eliminate the need to handle cash and aid in providing background information on prospective riders and drivers. New "car services" such as Uber, Lyft and Sidecar allow riders to use applications on their cellphones to request rides, pay fares and vet drivers. These services are more similar to taxis because they cater to single riders or small groups. However, one can envision a more bus-like service, carrying larger groups of passengers. Unlike a fixed-route bus, such a service could offer route deviations, as requested by a cellphone-carrying passenger.

Jitney opponents fear that without any regulations, jitneys will congest traffic, cannibalize existing transit and pose a safety hazard to passengers and passersby alike. Obviously, a proper balance of regulation and freedom will need to be found so the jitneys of the future will provide a safe and useful form of transportation.

CHAPTER 4

"A MILLIONAIRE TWICE"

O.R. Fuller's Motor Transit

I only have a third-grade education, but I've been a millionaire twice." These were the words of O.R. Fuller. While nearly forgotten today, he was one of the big names in Southern California transportation during the early twentieth century.

He started the Motor Transit bus company with a single route between Los Angeles and Fullerton in 1916. Within a decade, it had become the largest bus company in California.

He was also a leading automobile dealer. His dealerships sold a range of vehicles, from commercial trucks to luxury Auburn and Duesenberg automobiles.

During the Depression, he turned a neglected ranch into one of the largest dairy and poultry farms in Southern California, while converting his ranch house into a first-class guesthouse attracting celebrities from far and wide.

A BOY NAMED OLIVE

Olive Ransome Fuller was born in Smith Center, Kansas, on October 5, 1880. His parents, Charles Henry Fuller and Maud Spencer Fuller, divorced shortly after he was born. Charles moved to California, where, along with his brother, Ortus, he built a large ranching business covering many thousands of acres. In 1887, Maud remarried and settled on a farm south of Wichita.

Life in Kansas was rough in the 1880s and 1890s. Droughts and snowstorms killed cattle and ruined crops. Throughout these rough times, young Ransome's days were filled with the never-ending farm chores. He had to rise at 4:00 a.m. to work and was not finished until 8:00 p.m. This left little, if any, time for education.

O.R. ARRIVES IN CALIFORNIA

In 1898, when Ransome turned eighteen, he boarded a train to Los Angeles. Once there, O.R.—as he now liked to be called—lived with his father and worked at Pioneer Truck and Transfer. At the same time, he went to school, but apparently only for a few years, hence the "third-grade education" reference he often made much later in life.

He moved to the Olinda Ranch near Fullerton in 1905. Later that year, he married Agnes Nicolas. Although O.R. had little education, he had plenty of entrepreneurial ability. His first business was selling hay raised on the ranch. Then, with his brother-in-law, Peter, he opened the Eureka Livery Stables in Fullerton. O.R. also sold horses and mules and became a sales agent for a laundry, a wheat mill and a cement plant. He led a busy civic life as a member of the chamber of commerce. Hunting trips and horse races filled his leisure hours.

The automobile age arrived in Fullerton in about 1907. O.R. became Fullerton's Cadillac dealer, turning the Eureka Stables into the Eureka Stables and Garage. He loved to drive all over Southern California in a Cadillac.

PIONEER AUTO COMPANY

In April 1909, O.R. sold the Cadillac dealership and moved back to Los Angeles. For about a year, he worked at Pioneer Truck and Transfer, owned by his father and his uncle, Ortus. He started the Pioneer Commercial Auto Company in 1911, selling Reliance and White trucks along with Stephens automobiles. He especially liked the Stephens Salient Six model and would take it for pleasure drives around Southern California.

One day in 1913, O.R. reacquired two trucks from a failing business. Instead of trying to resell them, he decided to use them for Pioneer Truck and Transfer's suburban delivery service. The trucks proved to be moneymakers, as they were far more efficient than the horse-drawn wagons Pioneer still used.

O.R.'s wife, Agnes, became accustomed to life in Los Angeles, planning parties and becoming part of the city's social life. Unfortunately, she fell ill in late 1917 and passed away in March of the following year. In 1920, O.R. married Ione Wright, a young woman from Arizona.

MOTOR TRANSIT

Many early automobile owners used their vehicles as sources of income by offering rides and charging fares. As passenger traffic increased, drivers used larger cars and then switched to bus bodies on truck chassis. These buses, or "motor stages," operated along highways between cities and towns, competing with the railroads. California, with its mild weather and good roads, was ideal for the motor stage business.

O.R. ended up in the motor stage business by accident—literally. In 1916, he sold two White buses to the PE Stage Line, which connected Los Angeles and Anaheim via Whittier and Fullerton. After a bad accident, PE Stage Line went out of business. O.R. repossessed the buses and then decided to start a bus line of his own, assuming the route of the defunct company. He named his bus company White Bus Line, after the manufacturer of the two buses.

At first, these early bus lines operated without any regulation. Cities and counties applied their own taxes and regulations to the buses, creating a patchwork of rules. Adding to the problem was the occasional fly-by-night bus company.

The California Railroad Commission started regulating intercity buses on May 1, 1917. From then on, bus companies had to apply for, and be granted, a "certificate of public convenience and necessity" from the Commission. The agency set fares and rates, balancing the public's desire for low fares with the companies' need to make a reasonable profit. For bus lines operating between cities, the Commission's orders overruled city and county regulations, although local jurisdictions could still require permits.

Motor Transit bus. *Los Angeles Public Library Photo Collection.*

(The state constitution exempted from Commission jurisdiction any bus companies operating totally within an incorporated city or buses operated by a municipality.)

The Commission also managed competition among bus companies. According to its regulations, the first company to serve a given route had the exclusive right to pick up and drop off passengers along that route. Any subsequent companies wishing to serve the same route had to prove to the Commission that the existing service was inadequate to meet the public's need.

O.R., along with other bus company owners in California, formed the Motor Carriers' Association. This organization unified the bus companies politically, enabling them to lobby for favorable legislation and low tax rates. The association also worked with local and state government agencies to prevent unlicensed and unregulated drivers, known as "wildcats," from poaching passengers from the licensed bus lines.

STAGES ACROSS CALIFORNIA

In 1919, O.R. purchased the ARG and Clark Bus Lines, transforming White Bus Line from a one-route bus company to a network of routes stretching to Ontario, Riverside, San Bernardino and San Diego. He renamed the company to Motor Transit and, to avoid street congestion in central Los Angeles, built a bus terminal at Fifth and Los Angeles Streets. The terminal also served non–Motor Transit buses.

Motor Transit bus. *Courtesy Dorothy Peyton Gray Transportation Library.*

About one year later, O.R. acquired the El Dorado Stage Line, which connected Los Angeles and Bakersfield. The buses traveled over the Ridge Route, forty-eight miles of steep grades and hairpin turns. Running time between the two cities was about ten hours.

Bakersfield, and its fast-growing petroleum business, provided plenty of riders. But the city also served as a connecting point to stages northbound to the San Joaquin Valley and the Bay Area. Motor Transit, along with Valley Transit (Bakersfield–Merced) and California Transit (Merced–Oakland), entered into a pooling arrangement. All three companies supplied vehicles; a Motor Transit driver would operate between Los Angeles and Bakersfield, where a Valley Transit driver would take over for the segment to Merced. Once there, drivers from California Transit would drive the bus to Oakland. Passengers wishing to continue to San Francisco could take a ferry.

Working together, the companies provided three daily round trips between Los Angeles and the Bay Area. A fourth trip was added in 1924. The fourth trip was known as the "Sun-Maid Limited," named after the raisin-growing cooperative. Passengers on this trip received a free box of Sun-Maid raisins.

THE MOUNTAIN DIVISION

O.R., who had grown up in flat Kansas, was especially fond of the mountains near San Bernardino. He envisioned Motor Transit bus routes serving Lake Arrowhead and Big Bear.

However, the Mountain Auto Line had served the San Bernardino mountain roads since 1912. Since the Commission would not allow him to operate a competing service, O.R. decided to buy the Mountain Auto Line. Max Green, owner of the bus line, sold it to Motor Transit in 1920. O.R. put Green in charge of Motor Transit's new Mountain Division. Eventually, Green became Motor Transit's passenger traffic manager.

The Mountain Division may have been more trouble than it was worth. Its buses required special gear ratios, making them useless on flat roads. Passenger travel dropped off tremendously in the winter months. Heavy snowfall closed roads, detouring buses through Victorville or even shutting down service entirely. The mountain routes survived because of the freight they carried, not from passenger fares. Freight, from newspapers to auto parts, was an important part of Motor Transit's operations on its non-mountain routes as well.

Motor Transit bus, Mountain Division. *Courtesy Dorothy Peyton Gray Transportation Library.*

OTHER ROUTES

Motor Transit acquired several other routes. Most of these were short, such as Pomona–Chino or Bakersfield–Taft. Longer routes served San Jacinto, Lancaster, Verdugo Hills and Victorville. Additionally, Motor Transit operated the City of Montebello's municipal bus route along Whittier Boulevard from 1928 to 1931.

In late 1922, O.R., along with several Hollywood business leaders, formed the Hollywood Motorbus Company. The company proposed several local bus routes in Hollywood and two routes to downtown Los Angeles. However, Los Angeles's Board of Public Utilities and Transportation strongly opposed any new bus companies serving the already congested central area, so the Hollywood Motorbus backers abandoned their effort.

If O.R. could not operate local buses in the city, at least he could make money selling buses to Pacific Electric and the Los Angeles Railway. The two rail companies bought several White buses for use on their jointly owned Los Angeles Motor Coach bus system, which served Wilshire Boulevard and other streets lacking rail. "Well, we feel a little bit puffed up ourselves over this record for we sold eighty-one White buses right here in Los Angeles to electric traction companies in one order," said O.R. "The Pacific Electric and the Los Angeles Railway Company divided the order, and are now using these White buses in their augmented combination tram and bus service." He also sold buses to Yosemite and Yellowstone National Parks.

O.R.'S AUTO BUSINESS

Along with Motor Transit, O.R. continued to manage his automobile and truck dealerships. Many automobile dealerships opened on "Automobile Row," or Figueroa Boulevard south of downtown. O.R. moved the Stephens dealership there in September 1917.

Business boomed as people bought trucks and buses. The White factory in Cleveland had trouble keeping up with orders. After receiving an especially large shipment, O.R. remarked, "Business was never better. If I could only get all the trucks I want from the factory I might draw at least one long breath."

O.R. became an authority on automobiles and Los Angeles's growing "car culture." He was often quoted in newspapers across California, advising motorists about engine maintenance and driving techniques. He admitted to being bewildered by the auto-related slang used by younger people in the mid-1920s. "A motor car nowadays may be a 'bus,' 'boat,' 'wagon,' 'jazz cart,' 'buggy,' 'job,' and a lot of other things," remarked the then forty-seven-year-old O.R. "Even the motorists of the fair sex use 'step on it' and 'heavy foot it' instead of different forms of the verb, speed."

The White Auto Company started selling Auburn automobiles in 1923. O.R. was especially fond of these cars, stating in a 1924 *Los Angeles Times* article, "For twenty-three years Auburn motor cars have earned a reputation among satisfied owners for long sturdy life, good performance and general high value at a reasonable price." The Auburns were so popular that the increase in business nearly overwhelmed O.R.

In 1928, O.R. renamed the White Auto Company to the Auburn-Fuller Corporation and opened dealerships in Hollywood and San Francisco.

THE TRI-STAGE MERGER

By 1926, passengers were facing a bewildering array of bus companies, fares and service area restrictions. In order to untie this Gordian knot, Motor Transit, California Transit and Pickwick Stages, under the guidance of the Commission, divided the market among themselves, each choosing a specific area and type of service.

Under this agreement, known as the "Tri-Stage Merger," Motor Transit gave up its long-distance routes to Lancaster, Bakersfield and San Diego and became a suburban bus line serving Los Angeles, Orange, Riverside and San Bernardino Counties. In exchange, Motor Transit gained the rights to carry local passengers anywhere in its system. Motor Transit sold its Bakersfield route to California Transit, which would from then on connect Northern and Southern California via the Central Valley. Pickwick, which had just absorbed the Orange County routes of Crown Stages, gave up local rights along its routes in exchange for long-distance service between Los Angeles and San Diego.

About this time, bus companies across the United States merged into the national Greyhound Lines system. Southern Pacific, Santa Fe and other railroads also entered the bus business, running buses to replace poorly performing train trips.

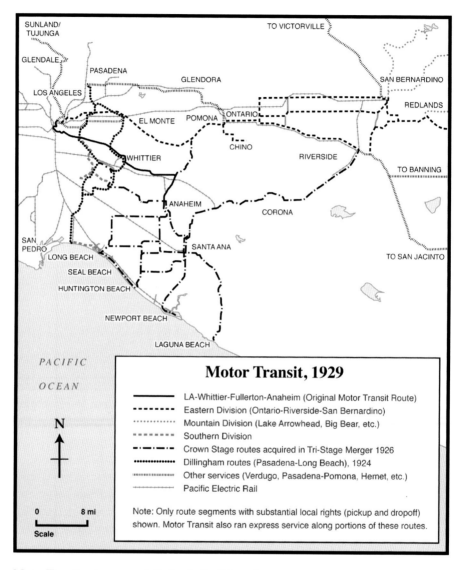

Motor Transit system map. *Author's collection/Mapcraft.*

In late 1929, O.R. sold Motor Transit to Pacific Transportation Securities, a holding company owned by Greyhound, Pickwick and Southern Pacific. O.R. received $3 million for the sale and remained on the board of directors of Motor Transit. The holding company, which renamed itself Pacific Greyhound Lines, later sold Motor Transit to Pacific Electric.

O.R.'s success with his auto dealerships, along with the sale of Motor Transit, enabled him and his family to move into a new, custom-built house in Los Feliz, east of Hollywood. The Fullers shared their new neighborhood with many actors and producers, such as Cecil B. DeMille, Julia Faye and William Fox. Los Feliz was the home of several business "movers and shakers" as well. The Chandlers, publishers of the *Los Angeles Times*, lived across the street; D.W. Pontius, president of the Pacific Electric (O.R.'s former competitor), also lived nearby.

PE, now controlling rather than competing with Motor Transit, shortened or discontinued rail lines in places where Motor Transit provided faster or more direct service. PE curtailed some of the less productive bus routes and sold the Mountain Division back to Max Green.

O.R. and E.L.

O.R.'s successful Auburn dealerships attracted the attention of Errett Lobban Cord, owner of the Auburn Automobile Company. Cord had also started in the automobile business at a young age. In 1924, he had bought the struggling Auburn with a low-ball, take-it-or-leave-it offer. Although his business tactics alienated many people, Cord had made Auburn profitable by 1926. Cord also acquired several companies, including Stinson Aircraft, Duesenberg Automobiles and Lycoming automobile and aircraft engines.

Cord, as enthusiastic about airplanes as he was about automobiles, entered the airline business in 1930. Century Airlines served the Midwest from a Chicago hub; Century Pacific flew from Grand Central Airport in Glendale to San Diego, Bakersfield and San Francisco. Both airlines used ten-passenger Stinson aircraft.

O.R. and Cord went into business together. Cord bought an interest in O.R.'s Auburn dealership and moved it from Figueroa Street into a new Art Deco building on Wilshire Boulevard, across the street from the Ambassador Hotel. Cord appointed O.R. president of Century Pacific.

Cord insisted that his employees work long hours at low wages. It was no different for the Century pilots, whom Cord considered "glorified chauffeurs" and paid at about half the normal rate. At first, the pilots were glad to have any job they could get and suffered in silence. But when Cord announced further wage cuts in 1931, the Chicago-based pilots went on strike.

Auburn-Fuller Company building, Wilshire & Mariposa, Los Angeles, 1932. *Los Angeles Examiner Collection, Department of Special Collections, University of Southern California.*

Cord kept expenses low, not only to compete with rail fares but also to offer a low bid on a U.S. Post Office airmail contract. However, Cord's business practices made him no friends with the government. U.S. Post Office officials noted that the pilots were so demoralized they flew unsafely, threatening the stability of the entire airline network. During the strike, Cord often referred to the striking pilots as "Reds" and "Communists," offending other government officials enough to prevent him from ever receiving another airmail contract.

Relations between Cord and O.R., who had initially admired each other, deteriorated. O.R. questioned Cord's treatment of the Century pilots, the Auburn factory workers and the Auburn dealers. Cord forced dealers to stock impractical, poorly selling models and balked at providing repairs when those cars developed mechanical problems.

1932: It Was a Very Bad Year

For O.R., 1932 was a far cry from the good times of 1929. On January 29, a Century Pacific airplane crashed in the mountains south of Bakersfield, killing all aboard. Because of bad weather and rough terrain, five days passed before the victims were found. Although Motor Transit buses had been involved in the occasional accident, nothing as serious as this had ever happened while O.R. owned the bus company.

In May, O.R. received a letter threatening him with death unless he provided $50,000. O.R. promptly turned the letter over to the police. Detectives determined that it was O.R.'s former chauffeur, recently terminated from employment, who had sent the letter. The ex-employee was quickly arrested.

By mid-year, Century Pacific Airlines had gone out of business, and Auburn-Fuller went into receivership. Much of O.R.'s wealth was in stocks, which were by now nearly worthless. He did not bother to attend the Century Pacific dissolution hearing on July 13, where Cord and his lawyers tried to prevent O.R. from taking his share of airline stock.

At year's end, O.R. decided to retire from the business world, leave Los Feliz and live on his ranch near Corona. However, this would not be a leisurely retirement; there would be much hard work to be done on the ranch so it could financially support his family.

Back to the Ranch

O.R.'s Eastvale ranch, three thousand acres six miles north of Corona, had been in the family since the 1870s. The Fuller brothers raised horses for Pioneer Truck and Transfer. As motor trucks replaced horse-drawn wagons, Charles Fuller gave less and less attention to the ranch, finally passing it on to O.R. in 1925.

O.R. expanded the ranch by purchasing adjacent property until it grew to five thousand acres. He leased an additional two thousand acres near the Santa Ana River, making it the largest ranch in the area.

The Fuller family enjoyed spending weekends at the ranch. In 1927, they built an elaborate ranch house, named Casa Orone (combining O.R. and Ione). It was lavishly appointed with Italian woodcarvings, Spanish rugs and other fine furnishings. And now it was going to be their permanent home, far away from the glamour of Los Feliz.

O.R., remembering his boyhood on that Kansas farm, started a dairy and a poultry farm. Within a few years, the Fuller Rancho had become the largest turkey farm in Southern California. Fuller Rancho trucks delivered milk and eggs all over Southern California. O.R. opened the Fuller Rancho Market, a drive-up grocery store, in Pomona.

For additional income, the Fullers opened Casa Orone as a guest ranch in 1937. Rooms were added to the house until there was space for twenty-five guests.

The Fuller Guest Rancho offered horseback riding, boating in the river, swimming pools, a fine restaurant and a comfortable lounge. There was also illegal gambling, with card tables and slot machines designed to be quickly hidden if law enforcement agents came calling. O.R. himself loved to gamble and often spent many hours playing poker.

Life at the Guest Rancho seemed like one big party lasting for days. Celebrities such as W.C. Fields, Groucho Marx, Spencer Tracy and Red Skelton were frequent guests. The Guest Rancho hosted many weddings, luncheons and business meetings.

In 1938, O.R. subdivided the ranch and sold lots with river views. One of the first purchasers was actor Charles Grapewin, who claimed to have won it from O.R. in a poker game. The street near his former property is still named Grapewin Street.

During World War II, medical staff and patients from the nearby Naval Hospital (Norconian Hotel) visited the Guest Rancho for relaxation, while German prisoners of war worked the fields.

O.R. passed away in 1946, and the Guest Rancho closed one year later. Ione remarried and continued living at the ranch until her death in 1951. Shortly thereafter, the ranch was purchased by a local dairyman. Casa Orone became a senior citizens residence and then was used as a home for wayward youth until it was demolished in 2004. Most of O.R.'s Eastvale ranch is now suburbia, covered with tract homes and shopping centers, although a few dairy farms still operate. In June 2010, residents voted to make Eastvale an incorporated city.

EPILOGUE

By 1939, the name Motor Transit had disappeared from the buses, and the routes were simply known as Pacific Electric. The basic structure of Motor Transit's bus route network remained intact through the decades as Metropolitan Coach Lines, Los Angeles Metropolitan Transit Authority, Southern California Rapid Transit District and Los Angeles County Metropolitan Transit Authority (MTA or "Metro") operated the buses. Some routes changed as Southern California's freeways opened, and longer routes used them to speed service. In the mid-'70s, the outlying counties (Orange, Riverside and San Bernardino) formed their own transit agencies and took over the portions of bus routes in their jurisdictions; Foothill Transit did the same for eastern Los Angeles County in the late 1980s.

Although the automobile business is usually assumed to be hostile to public transit, other automobile entrepreneurs have unwittingly followed O.R.'s lead in providing public transportation. J. Chapman Morris, a Chevrolet dealer in Fillmore, California, founded Fillmore Area Transit Corporation (FATCO) in 1973. FATCO provides local service in and around the city of Fillmore to this day. More recently, Yosuf Maiwandi, a Monrovia-based auto mechanic, implemented the San Gabriel Valley Transit Authority, offering free rides to the elderly and disabled, in the early 2000s.

CHAPTER 5

THE WAY TO TERMINAL ISLAND

The San Pedro Harbor Ferry and the
Vincent Thomas Bridge

T he Vincent Thomas Bridge's 6,000-foot span, arching 185 feet above Los Angeles Harbor, has efficiently carried traffic between San Pedro and Terminal Island since November 1963. Previously, anyone needing to cross the harbor had to travel the long way around the bay or take a ferry.

SAN PEDRO'S EARLY FERRIES

A small settlement near San Pedro Bay since 1769 was little more than a smugglers' cove until the Mexican-American War ended in 1848. Once the land became part of the United States, Americans migrated westward to California.

Delaware-born Phineas Banning settled north of the bay, in an area now known as Wilmington, in 1851. He developed stagecoach and wagon lines, and eventually a railroad, between the bay and Los Angeles. He also owned several small boats, or "lighters," used to load and unload passengers and freight from larger steamships. Lighters also crossed the one-thousand-foot channel between San Pedro and Rattlesnake Island, the largest island in San Pedro Bay.

East San Pedro, a resort village and artists' colony, appeared on Rattlesnake Island in the 1870s. Martin Lindskow, a Danish immigrant, provided the first known dedicated ferry service between San Pedro and the island, using a rowboat. Lindskow operated the ferry on an "on-call" basis. If the boat was on the opposite shore, the prospective passenger would shout across the channel to get the boatman's attention.

In 1887, Irish immigrant Michael Duffy obtained a twenty-year ferry franchise from the County of Los Angeles. Duffy's gasoline-powered launches, each named after one of his children (Blanche, Dora, Ida, George and Elise), connected the mainland with a bathhouse on the island.

Southern Pacific acquired Banning's railroad in 1873 and extended it from Wilmington to San Pedro. The Los Angeles Terminal Island Railway extended its tracks to Rattlesnake Island in 1891, renaming it Terminal Island. Since each railroad ended on opposite sides of the channel, ferryboats were needed to bring passengers to their destinations. This business soon overwhelmed Duffy's launches, and by 1899, the railroads were providing their own ferry services.

The San Pedro Transportation Company

Railroad companies pressured the County of Los Angeles to improve ferry service. Frank Garbutt, a politically powerful shipbuilder, along with the railroads, convinced the Los Angeles County Board of Supervisors to give him the ferry franchise. In a November 1906 closed-door meeting, the supervisors voted to transfer the franchise from Duffy to Garbutt. Duffy reluctantly sold his boats to Garbutt, who, along with Matt J. Walsh, formed the San Pedro Transportation Company.

San Pedro Bay became Los Angeles's official harbor in 1899. The Port of Los Angeles and the Los Angeles Harbor Commission were founded in 1907. The citizens of San Pedro and Wilmington voted to allow Los Angeles to annex their cities in 1909, after being promised numerous civic improvements, including a municipal ferry. However, under pressure from Garbutt, the city "forgot" its promise and renewed SPTC's franchises.

San Pedro and Terminal Island grew in population. Tuna canneries replaced beach resorts, and fishermen moved into houses previously occupied by artists and tourists. Japanese immigrants settled in a small village, which they called Furusato, on the island. Cannery workers and others filled the ferries.

Team Ferry. Courtesy San Pedro Bay Historical Society.

To meet the increased demand, SPTC built two foot ferries, *Peer* and *Real*, in 1912. Two years later came the sixty-foot-long *TF*, or *Team Ferry*. It could carry eight horse-and-wagon teams, although automobiles and trucks were rapidly replacing horses and wagons. SPTC built its last two boats in 1918. The *MJW* (named after SPTC founder Matt J. Walsh) and the *Ace* were the biggest foot ferries in the fleet at fifty-three and fifty-seven feet, respectively.

But the new boats were unsatisfactory. The *MJW* and the *Ace* failed to protect passengers against sea spray and bad weather, while the *Team Ferry* could only carry a few vehicles at a time and ran limited hours. When *TF* was idle, prospective passengers had to drive to Wilmington and cross a drawbridge to reach Terminal Island.

The SPTC became known as the "Toonerville Ferry," after the badly run trolley of the *Toonerville Folks* comic strip. Businessmen complained about the difficulties in moving trucks between San Pedro and Terminal Island and the reluctance of the Harbor Commission to improve ferry service. In 1929, Harbor Commission president Walter B. Allen admitted that the ferry service was "an utter disgrace to the port."

At the Harbor Commission meeting on May 2, 1934, San Pedro Chamber of Commerce president Leslie Mott stated, "Lack of adequate ferry service is the only unfilled promise made to San Pedro by Los Angeles in the consolidation agreement of 1909. We feel that this, the second port in the United States, cannot afford any longer to put up with this type of service." But the Commission, fearing that a municipal ferry would be expensive to run, balked.

LOS ANGELES KEEPS ITS PROMISE

Although Garbutt warned that a municipal ferry would require increased taxes, and also continued to defend the SPTC, by 1940, San Pedrans had had enough. They insisted that Los Angeles fulfill its 1909 promise. Under pressure from the San Pedro Chamber of Commerce and other groups, the Harbor Commission started searching for suitable vessels for the municipal ferry. By this time, World War II was raging in Europe and the Pacific, keeping all the shipbuilders occupied. A new ferry was out of the question. A used boat would have to do.

The Commission looked at several vessels before deciding on the 120-foot-long *Mercer*, docked unused in Lake Washington, near Seattle.

The *Mercer* was originally the *MV Vashon Island*. Built in 1916, it was the first double-ended vehicle ferry in service between Seattle and Vashon Island. By 1921, newer boats were providing the Seattle–Vashon Island service, and the *MV Vashon Island* was renamed *Mercer* and served Lake Washington between Seattle and Mercer Island.

A new floating bridge opened in 1939, eliminating the need for the *Mercer*. The Commission bought the ferry in 1941 for $5,500 and towed it to San

Islander ferry. *Courtesy San Pedro Bay Historical Society.*

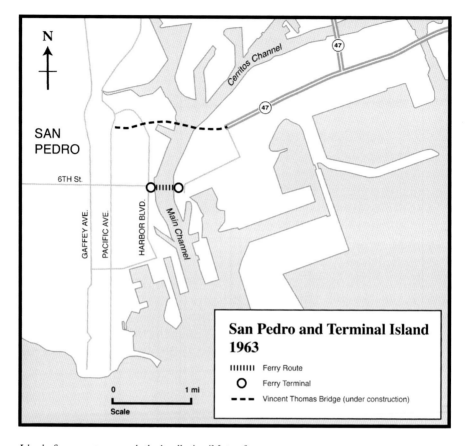

Islander ferry route map. *Author's collection/Mapcraft.*

Pedro. Once the ferry arrived, the Commission spent $40,000 repairing it and built two new ferry terminals in San Pedro and on Terminal Island.

The Commission held a "Name the Ferry" contest; out of 370 entries, 2 entrants picked the name "Islander" and shared a twenty-dollar prize. A dedication ceremony for the *Islander* was held on August 8, 1941. The ferry's trial run went well, other than a minor collision with a small sandbar.

Regular service started September 2. The first trip, carrying one hundred passengers and eight automobiles, left San Pedro at 6:00 a.m. Three minutes and thirty seconds later, the ferry reached Terminal Island. The passenger loading ramps were not ready until a month later, requiring foot passengers to use the car ramps. Still, the *Islander*, capable of carrying four hundred passengers and twenty-six cars, was an improvement over the SPTC boats.

The ferry sailed every twenty minutes, between 6:00 a.m. and midnight. In the wee hours, or when the *Islander* was being maintained, the *Ace* provided passenger-only service. The *TF* and *MJW* worked standby duty only until they were auctioned in 1959.

The December 7, 1941 attack on Pearl Harbor plunged the United States into World War II. San Pedro and Terminal Island buzzed with military activity. The Japanese and Japanese Americans on the island were removed and sent to internment camps; their village was plundered and bulldozed. Soldiers, sailors and shipyard workers joined the fishermen and cannery employees on the trips across the channel. At shift-change times, an additional one thousand passengers would crowd onto the *Islander*'s car deck.

San Pedro had finally received its long-promised municipal ferry. But some people felt that a more efficient way of moving people and vehicles across the harbor was needed.

VINCENT THOMAS

"I've lived in San Pedro nearly all my life, and I hate Los Angeles!" When Vincent Thomas spoke these words during his campaign for California State Assembly in 1940, he received thunderous applause.

Vincent Thomas, born in Pass Christian, Mississippi, in 1908, came to San Pedro in 1918 when his father landed a job with the Southern Pacific Railroad. Both his parents died a few years after arriving, forcing young Vincent to work as a paperboy to support his younger siblings. Life on the streets of San Pedro was rough, and Vincent had to fight other paperboys to maintain his territory. Street fighting led to amateur boxing and an athletic scholarship at Santa Clara University. After graduating, he attended law school but failed the bar exam. In 1940, as he was contemplating a career with the merchant marine, Fred Reaves, the California assemblyman for the San Pedro area, suddenly died. Several of Thomas's former high school classmates persuaded him to run for the vacant position. Thomas campaigned and won, getting three times as many votes as his closest opponent.

Once in office, the new assemblyman wrote several bills and resolutions reflecting San Pedrans' distrust of the City of Los Angeles and their desire to make San Pedro an independent city. On January 8, 1947, Thomas introduced a bill allowing San Pedro to secede from Los Angeles. Unfortunately, support for secession was not as great as he had thought. Mayor Fletcher Bowron made matters worse by insinuating that Communists were behind the secession movement. Bowron later apologized for the remark, but the damage was done; several assemblymen rescinded their support for the bill.

TUBE OR BRIDGE

In 1947, Thomas announced his desire to replace the ferry with a roadway crossing, an idea discussed since 1928. The crossing could be a bridge high enough to accommodate ships passing under it. Or it could be a less expensive underwater tube, similar to the one opened in 1924 between Oakland and Alameda.

Throughout the 1930s, the San Pedro Chamber of Commerce advocated a tube crossing. So did Los Angeles mayors John C. Porter, Frank Shaw and Fletcher Bowron during their respective periods in office. In 1937, California state senator Culbert Olsen introduced a bill funding a tunnel between San Pedro and Terminal Island, but the bill died in committee.

Wartime and postwar activities increased traffic to San Pedro and Terminal Island. The California Division of Highways, along with the U.S. Army, reopened discussions about an underwater traffic tube.

Starting in March 1948, Thomas wrote several resolutions and bills calling for a study of a tube crossing. Although the Division of Highways determined that a tube would be feasible to build, funds would not be allocated until 1953.

MONEY-LOSING FERRY

After the war, only cannery workers, fishermen and a few tourists constituted the ferry's ridership. Shipyard workers moved to Long Beach and commuted to Terminal Island via a floating bridge built during the war. Ferry use dropped.

The 1916-built *Islander* was reliable but expensive to maintain, costing nearly $100,000 per year to operate by 1951. As fares were only collected on trips to Terminal Island, commuters carpooled to work on the island and then rode the ferry home for free. The Commission increased fares to five cents each way for foot passengers; autos were charged twenty-five cents. Four years later, fares rose to ten cents for foot passengers and thirty cents per auto.

The ferry crew, demanding a pay raise, went on a three-day strike on August 12, 1951. Their union barred a local water taxi company from offering replacement service. Terminal Island Transit ran buses from San Pedro to Terminal Island, but the ride took at least forty-five minutes.

A different kind of "strike" occurred on February 6, 1954. At 7:16 a.m., the *Islander* left San Pedro for Terminal Island in heavy fog, carrying one hundred passengers. The pilot sounded a "fog signal," several five-second-long blasts on the ferry's whistle, as it crossed the harbor. Suddenly, a Union Oil tanker loomed out of the fog. The pilot threw the engines into full reverse power but was unable to slow down enough to avoid colliding with the tanker. The force of the collision knocked down a passenger standing on the auto deck, seriously injuring him. The collision could have been much worse, since the tanker contained highly flammable aviation gasoline.

The City of Los Angeles sued Union Oil for damages to the ferry. Because this was considered an admiralty case, it was moved from municipal to federal court. The proceedings determined that the tanker's crew neither responded to the *Islander*'s fog signals nor sent appropriate signals of its own. On June 26, 1956, the judge ruled in favor of the city, ordering Union Oil to pay $7,945 in damages.

Let's Build a Bridge

In 1953, Governor Earl Warren signed a bill appropriating $200,000 for engineering studies. The studies determined that a four-lane bridge would only cost 20 percent more than a two-lane tube. In July 1957, the governor signed a Thomas-authored bill allowing a choice of bridge or tube. Thomas's final bill, signed by the governor on April 15, 1958, authorized a $20 million, four-lane bridge, paid for by a combination of tolls and bonds.

Discussion arose about the new bridge's name. Because the bridge was to be painted green, some people suggested "Green Gate," corresponding to San Francisco's Golden Gate Bridge. Thomas himself preferred "Angel's Gate." However, the San Pedro Chamber of Commerce and other groups strongly felt that the bridge should be named after Thomas. Initially, Thomas was opposed. "Things like that happen after you are dead," he remarked. But support for naming the bridge after Thomas increased, and on June 19, 1961, the assembly voted to name the bridge the Vincent Thomas Bridge.

Groundbreaking took place on July 21, 1961. Workers drove supports for the bridge's towers into the ground. Then they welded the towers together. This was the first suspension bridge in the United States with welded, not riveted, towers. Once the towers were in place, workers spun together the thirteen-inch-thick steel suspension cables. Next came the roadbed frame, on which the concrete roadbed was poured.

As the bridge neared completion, officials announced that November 15, 1963, would be the opening date. A dedication ceremony was held on September 28, during San Pedro's annual Fisherman's Fiesta. The ceremony included a two-hour parade from San Pedro to the Harbor Boulevard bridge approach. Officials from the Harbor Commission, the City of Los Angeles and the San Pedro Chamber of Commerce saluted Thomas in their speeches as a squadron of navy jet fighters flew overhead.

GOODBYE FERRY, HELLO BRIDGE

The *Islander*'s last run would be at midnight, November 15, 1963, when the bridge would open. But the chamber of commerce was not willing to let the *Islander* just sail off into oblivion. Instead, the chamber planned a "wake" for the ferry's final run.

Only four hundred tickets, the passenger capacity of the *Islander*, would be sold. Tickets, which included dinner, the ferry ride, the ribbon-cutting ceremony and the bridge toll payment, sold out quickly in the first half of November. Ferry ridership suddenly increased as longtime passengers unable to buy tickets, along with tourists, took "one last ride."

At both the dinner and on the ferry, guests—some teary-eyed, others clutching bits and pieces of the ferry as souvenirs—told colorful tales about their experiences on the *Islander*. They recalled the floating craps games on

SOUVENIR TICKET
Commemorating

Last Ferry Ride

ABOARD "THE ISLANDER"
SAN PEDRO — TERMINAL ISLAND
N.º 386   NOVEMBER 14, 1963   DONATION $10.00

The last ferry ride ticket. *Courtesy San Pedro Bay Historical Society.*

board; fortunes could change hands quickly within the three-minute crossing time. They remembered the drunks fighting on board. If necessary, the crew would sound six long whistle blasts, signaling every policeman in San Pedro to meet the ferry. Some even remembered a strange lady who would strip naked and jump overboard almost every night.

Instead of following its usual route, the *Islander* traveled north, passed under the new bridge and entered Cerritos Channel, along the north side of the island. At the Badger Street drawbridge, the ferry captain blew the horn, signaling the drawbridge to open. Then the *Islander* proceeded toward Long Beach Harbor, waited there a few minutes and then returned to San Pedro Bay.

At 10:45 p.m., the ferry arrived at San Pedro. Everyone deboarded, got into their cars and drove in a caravan, honking their horns, to the bridge approach. Thomas, along with his family and various civic and business leaders, led the caravan riding in a Terminal Island Transit bus.

A few moments before midnight, the caravan stopped at the bridge entrance. A ribbon stretched across the traffic lanes. Thomas and his entourage stepped off the bus and walked to the ribbon. He snipped the

Vincent Thomas at the bridge opening ceremony. *Courtesy San Pedro Bay Historical Society.*

ribbon with a giant pair of wooden scissors. Then the caravan, again led by Thomas's bus and flanked by motorcycle officers, crossed the bridge. Once on Terminal Island, Thomas again hopped out of the bus and paid the first toll. The bridge was now open to the public.

After ferry service ended, the Commission sold both ferries. The *Ace* served as a harbor boat for a few years. In 1971, microbiologist Ronald DiSalvo bought the ferry and made it into a beautiful luxury houseboat.

The *Islander*'s "afterlife" was not as bright. It became a fishing barge off Belmont Shore. On Christmas Day 1974, a fire broke out in its engine. The ferry burned to the waterline and capsized.

Although the Terminal Island ferry terminal was torn down, the terminal building in San Pedro stayed intact. The Harbor Department occupied the building until 1976, when it was restored by the citizens of San Pedro and designated a historic monument. Since 1979, it has housed the Los Angeles Maritime Museum.

WE STILL WANT A FERRY

The Vincent Thomas Bridge provided the ultimate convenience—for drivers. Instead of waiting in a ferry line, drivers could travel across the bay in a few minutes.

But for those without cars, including most of the cannery workers, the bridge was anything but convenient. No sidewalk was provided, and pedestrians were prohibited. Non-drivers had to use Terminal Island Transit buses, which took longer than the ferry, charged higher fares and often were caught in traffic backups.

The ferry's absence hurt the neighborhood near the ferry terminal. Businesses depending on foot traffic from the ferry closed, and the area declined.

A group of San Pedrans started a "bring back the ferry" movement in 1968. Sylvia Zankich, bail bondswoman and "honorary mayor" of San Pedro, collected five thousand signatures on a petition for a passenger-only ferry between San Pedro and Terminal Island. Old ferry tokens were sold as souvenirs to finance the campaign.

The Harbor Commission, however, was not interested. State laws prohibited ferries, even passenger-only ferries, from competing with toll bridges with unpaid bonds. The Commission, recalling the years of money-losing ferry service, strongly doubted that any private company would be interested in restoring ferry service.

EMBRACING THE BRIDGE, RESTORING THE FERRY

The Vincent Thomas Bridge has become a symbol of San Pedro and Los Angeles Harbor. It has appeared in movies, was used in local marathons and bike races and, sadly, has seen its share of suicides. The bridge has withstood high winds; major earthquakes in 1971, 1987 and 1994; post-9/11 terrorism concerns; and even a minor collision with a ship in 2006.

When the bridge opened, a twenty-five-cent toll was collected each way at the Terminal Island tollbooth. In 1983, toll-takers collected fifty cents westbound only, to avoid backups on the bridge. Until his death in 1980, Thomas himself would often drive across "his" bridge and chat with the toll-takers. By 2000, enough money had been collected to pay the bonds, and the toll was abolished.

Islander, Ace and the Vincent Thomas Bridge. *Courtesy San Pedro Bay Historical Society.*

While early detractors called the bridge a "white elephant" and a "bridge to nowhere," the steady hum of more than thirty-two thousand daily vehicles on the span speaks otherwise. Without the bridge, the ports of Los Angeles and Long Beach could have never become the busiest ports in the United States.

In October 2009, the Port of Los Angeles proposed an extensive restoration of the San Pedro waterfront, including "water taxi" stops along the shoreline in San Pedro and perhaps to Wilmington—but not to Terminal Island.

A new ferry service would serve a Terminal Island substantially different from the days of the *Islander* and the *Ace*. The last shipyard closed in 1989, and the last cannery shut down in 2001; container facilities, recycling yards and the Federal Correctional Institution dominate. A former cannery is undergoing historic preservation; if it becomes a museum, it might spark an interest in restoring a cross-channel ferry.

CHAPTER 6

BRUNNER, RINDGE, HOYME AND HENDLER

Transportation Pioneers of the Malibu

The scenic Pacific Coast Highway (PCH) provides an enjoyable drive—when it is not congested—along the Malibu coast between Santa Monica and Oxnard. However, few who travel PCH know the long and complicated history of the road. Even fewer know about the attempts to provide public transportation along the highway.

Fredrick and May Rindge, who owned the land comprising Malibu, fought vigorously against the highway crossing their property in the early twentieth century. Once the Rindges lost their battle and the road opened to the public in 1929, entrepreneurs such as Francis Brunner, Major Robert Hoyme and Frank Hendler attempted, with varying success, to provide bus service along PCH.

SOUTHERN CALIFORNIA'S PRETTIEST DRIVE

Francis Brunner, the son of Rudolf Brunner and Clara Schroff Brunner, was born on December 17, 1899, in Santa Monica. In his late teens, he worked as a copy reader for the *Los Angeles Examiner*. He left Santa Monica in 1919 to attend Pomona College and the University of Michigan. He returned to Santa Monica in 1923 and worked at the *Los Angeles Herald* as a copy editor.

Southern California's Prettiest Drive

OFFICIAL TIME TABLE *and*
SCHEDULE OF FARES

Castle Rock, on the coast highway north of Santa Monica, a part of the scenic route traversed by the Topanga and Las Flores Canyon Stages

Topanga and Las Flores Canyon Stages

Leave from Santa Monica Opposite
P. E. Railway Station

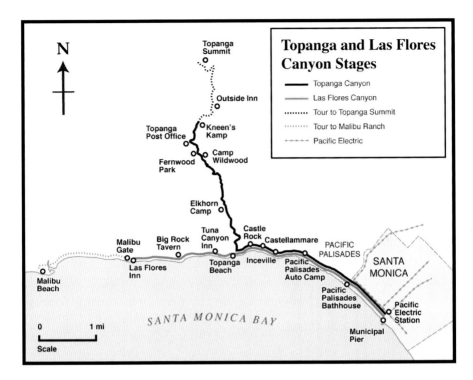

Opposite: Southern California's "Prettiest Drive" schedule pamphlet. *Courtesy Topanga Historical Society.*

Above: Topanga and Las Flores Canyon Stages, 1925. *Author's collection/Mapcraft.*

In November 1924, Brunner purchased the Topanga and Las Flores Canyon Stages bus line from Topanga Canyon pioneer Thomas Cheney for $1,200. All trips originated at the Santa Monica Pacific Electric station; three daily round trips went to Topanga Canyon and two to Las Flores Canyon.

Brunner marketed the bus line as "Southern California's Prettiest Drive." Although the bus line was primarily intended for sightseeing, Brunner sold one-way fares for those people staying at one of the numerous inns or campgrounds along the routes. A trip through the canyons, Brunner said, could improve one's appetite, relax the nerves and cure the "blues." Onboard the Stages, Brunner intoned, "the only 'blues' are the blues of rollicking ocean waves, the blues of clearest skies, and the blues of range on range of distant mountains."

The first "buses" on the Las Flores and Topanga routes were Dodge and Packard automobiles, "stretched" to accommodate more passengers.

In 1926, Brunner bought a Graham Brothers coach, primarily to carry schoolchildren from Topanga Canyon to Santa Monica, but it was also used on his regular routes.

Brunner operated tours to the Topanga Summit, which provided an expansive view of the San Fernando Valley. Another tour traveled the coast road past Las Flores Canyon and through the Malibu Ranch. He anticipated the construction of a public highway through the ranch. Like many of his passengers, he wondered, "What lies over the hill beyond the end of the paved road?"

Through the Malibu Ranch

This piece of paradise, known as the Malibu Ranch (or Rancho Topanga Malibu Sequit), was mostly off limits to the general public. Malibu, named after the Chumash word for "loud surf," was originally granted by the Spanish government to Jose Bartolome Tapia in 1805. The ranch passed through several hands before Fredrick and May Rindge of Boston bought it in 1892.

Fredrick and May loved their ranch. In 1898, Fredrick wrote a book, *Happy Days in Southern California*, extolling the virtues of the Malibu Ranch, comparing it to the Italian Rivera and proposing a road for leisure trips in horse-drawn carriages.

The Rindges permitted a few tenants to live on the ranch. Otherwise, public access was severely restricted. The main road through the ranch remained closed; tenants and other travelers had to use a path along the beach. During high tides, the path was impassable, and those traveling to and from their homes often had to wait several hours until the ocean receded.

In the late 1890s, the Southern Pacific Railway planned to extend its line from Santa Monica to Oxnard through the Malibu Ranch. Fredrick Rindge did not want Southern Pacific "invading" his land, and he knew that if there were already a railroad on the ranch, Southern Pacific would be less likely to apply eminent domain condemnation proceedings. In 1903, he formed the Hueneme, Malibu and Port Los Angeles Railway Company and began construction on the Malibu Ranch's own rail line.

The sudden death of Fredrick in 1905 changed nothing. May continued to keep the public out and worked to prevent a public highway from being

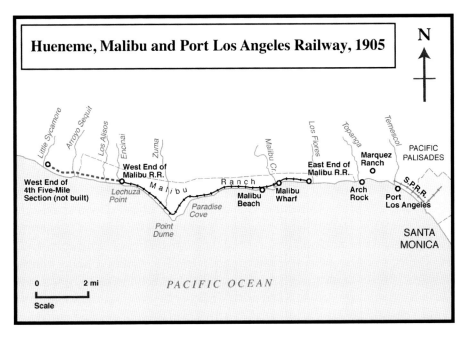

Hueneme, Malibu and Port Los Angeles Railway. *Adapted from David F. Myrick, "The Determined Mrs. Rindge and Her Legendary Railroad,"* Ventura County Historical Society Quarterly *41, no. 3/Mapcraft.*

built through the ranch. Armed men on horseback met trespassers and shooed them off the property. Her strong insistence that the public stay off her ranch, and her even stronger actions to keep people away, earned her the title "Queen of the Malibu."

May took charge of the Hueneme, Malibu and Port Los Angeles, making her one of the few women in history to own a railroad. By 1908, she had built about fifteen miles of railroad along the shore between Las Flores Canyon and Encinal Canyon, passing via Point Dume. It mostly carried agricultural products and supplies to and from the pier. On rare occasions, it carried ranch visitors. However, the railroad was never extended off the ranch; doing so would require negotiating with the Southern Pacific on the east end. Extending tracks west to Oxnard involved cooperation with the Broome family, who guarded their ranch as jealously, if not more so, than the Rindges did theirs.

Rindge used legal and extralegal means to keep interlopers, including County of Los Angeles officials, off the ranch. In courtroom hearings, Rindge testified that settlers and trespassers harassed her family, started fires and stole cattle. The courts sided with the county, but when road builders started work, they were met by men with guns. Once, Rindge had parts of the road near the gates blown up with dynamite.

The legal battle went to the United States Supreme Court in 1923. In the case *Rindge Company v. Los Angeles County*, the court affirmed the county's right to use eminent domain to build a public road through the ranch.

The State of California proceeded to condemn a right-of-way through the ranch for a highway in 1927. Much of the right-of-way was formerly that of the railroad, which had been damaged by storms in 1914 and 1916. On June 29, 1929, PCH, then known as the Roosevelt Highway, opened to the public. Governor Clement C. Young cut a ceremonial ribbon across the road, and traffic started flowing through the formerly "forbidden" property.

Because her legal battles nearly bankrupted her, Rindge decided to start subdividing her ranch. A few small lots became the Malibu Colony, which attracted movie stars in search of privacy. May Rindge passed away on March 12, 1941, in Los Angeles, away from her beloved Malibu Ranch. As for the Malibu railroad, nearly all of the track had been taken up and sold for scrap by the mid-1930s. However, forgotten pieces of rail have occasionally popped up out of the pavement as recently as the mid-1970s.

BRUNNER GOES TO OXNARD

Before the Coast Road even opened, bus companies big and small began planning to use it. The new road would shorten trips between Santa Monica and Oxnard, Ventura, Santa Barbara and San Francisco. No longer would passengers have to ride Pacific Electric into downtown Los Angeles and then transfer to a northbound train or bus. Instead, they could enjoy a shorter and more scenic ride along the coast.

Brunner saw the new road as his second opportunity to expand service. In 1926, he had filed an application with the California Railroad Commission for a certificate to run a bus service between downtown Los Angeles and Pacific Palisades via Beverly Boulevard. However, both Pacific Electric and the City of Los Angeles, thinking that Brunner lacked sufficient financial support to run the line, convinced him to transfer the certificate to Pacific Electric.

Brunner turned his full attention to obtaining a certificate to operate along the coast road. He formed a corporation called Santa Monica Mountain

Coach Line to operate both his existing routes and the new service. The Mountain Coach Line, using Studebaker buses, would run up to eight round trips every day between Santa Monica and Oxnard, making local stops along the way.

Four other companies proposed service via the new road. Southern Pacific's Pacific Coast Motor Coach Company proposed two round trips between Santa Monica and Oxnard. Pickwick Stages, the big statewide bus company, sought to extend its route from San Pedro to Oxnard, via Santa Monica. Another bus operator, confusingly named Motor Coach Company and headquartered in Lomita, planned to extend its Long Beach–Santa Monica route to San Francisco. Finally, Los Angeles and Oxnard Daily Express, a trucking firm, expressed interest in operating a bus linking Los Angeles, Santa Monica and Oxnard but failed to apply for a certificate from the Railroad Commission.

About a month before the road opened to the public, Brunner obtained permission from the California Highway Commission for a test drive. Studebaker supplied a luxurious, late-model parlor coach for the demonstration. On May 2, 1929, the bus arrived in Santa Monica at 10:00 a.m. Brunner—along with Santa Monica mayor Herman Michel, Studebaker representatives, other prominent citizens and the press— boarded the bus. At 10:30 a.m., the coach left Santa Monica and headed onto the coast highway for the trip to Oxnard.

Passengers relaxed in the comfortable seats and watched the scenery go by as the bus sped past Malibu Beach at up to seventy miles per hour. The road was in excellent condition, save for a few small landslides near Point Mugu. At 11:40 a.m., the bus arrived in Oxnard, where members of the local chamber of commerce greeted the travelers. Shortly thereafter, the bus continued on to Ventura, where it was met by city officials.

After a day of touring Ventura and Oxnard, Brunner and the others attended a meeting of the Oxnard Chamber of Commerce. He made a presentation promoting his proposed bus line, comparing it with the Pacific Coast Motor Coach Line's competing proposal. Southern Pacific planned to use these buses to connect passengers from Santa Monica to its trains in Oxnard.

"The S.P. plan is doomed to fail," declared Brunner. "Their buses will only go to Oxnard with but two trips a day. There is not enough revenue in that and it does not develop business. Besides, bus passengers do not travel on trains, or vice versa, so the S.P. plan of having Oxnard as a transfer point will never work."

Norman Robotman, a representative of the Pacific Coast Motor Coach Company, took notice as Brunner continued to describe his proposed Mountain Coach service. Upon questioning by Robotman, Brunner admitted that his Las Flores Canyon route was a money loser and that Santa Monica Mountain Coach was extremely underfunded, with only $700 in the bank.

After the meeting, Brunner and the others returned to Santa Monica via the Conejo Grade, Ventura Boulevard and Los Angeles.

HEARINGS AND REHEARINGS

At a series of Railroad Commission hearings in July 1929, representatives of Brunner's Santa Monica Mountain Coach, Pickwick Stages, Pacific Coast Motor Coach and the Lomita-based Motor Coach Company testified as to why the company they represented was most qualified to provide the Santa Monica–Oxnard route.

Because Brunner had no experience beyond the Topanga and Las Flores Canyon routes, the Commission was not confident in his ability to operate a more extensive service. Instead, the Commission awarded the certificates to the Motor Coach Company for service to San Francisco and to Pacific Coast Motor Coach for local service between Santa Monica and Oxnard.

However, the United States long-distance bus industry had been consolidating throughout 1929; smaller companies merged or were acquired by larger firms. In California, Southern Pacific's bus operations merged with Pickwick Stages to form Pacific Transportation Securities, which would eventually become Pacific Greyhound Lines.

In light of the changes in the bus industry, the Commission agreed to rehear the issue of Malibu bus service on December 3, 1929. This time, only Brunner's Santa Monica Mountain Coach, Pickwick and Motor Coach Company applied. Again, the hearings and testimony continued over several days. Pickwick representatives stated that the company planned to spend $1.25 million on one hundred new buses and that it was the most qualified of the four applicants to operate the Coast Highway service. This time, the Commission awarded the certificate for operations over the Coast Highway to Pickwick, again shutting Brunner out.

Brunner's Last Stand: Buses to the Palisades

The Pacific Land Company, which developed and sold land in the Pacific Palisades, had provided bus service between Santa Monica and the Palisades since the early 1920s. Originally intended to encourage purchase of real estate, the service was poorly patronized, and the company planned to cancel it.

Brunner bought the bus line in 1933, hoping that it would become profitable. Unfortunately, neither the Palisades route nor his service to Topanga and Las Flores Canyons made any money. Also, the schools had chosen another bus company to transport their students. Brunner needed a more stable source of income, as he had recently married and started a family.

In June 1935, Brunner sold all of his bus operations to the City of Santa Monica. The Santa Monica Municipal Bus Lines incorporated the Palisades route into its network but refused to continue service on the lightly used Las Flores and Topanga Canyon routes.

After Santa Monica acquired his bus line, Brunner sought employment as a bus driver. Instead, the city hired him to create a bus tour program. Brunner developed several guided tours to places such as the Los Angeles County Fair, Lake Arrowhead and the 1935 World's Fair in San Diego. By 1940, Santa Monica's bus tours were traveling as far as Arizona's Grand Canyon and Oregon's Crater Lake.

In 1941, Brunner became director of special tours for the Tanner Gray Line, a sightseeing bus company. The position was short-lived, however, as the United States' entry into World War II quickly put an end to luxuries such as guided bus tours. He entered the aircraft industry, eventually ending up at Hughes Aircraft, until he retired in the mid-1960s.

In his later years, Brunner, along with his wife, Barbara, helped develop a bus service bringing concertgoers to the Hollywood Bowl from various parts of Los Angeles County. Brunner, with the encouragement of his son, Robert F. Brunner, a composer with Walt Disney Studios, composed a Christmas song ("Here He Comes, Santa Claus"). Brunner died on September 18, 1981.

MAJOR HOYME'S SHORELINE TRANSIT

After World War II, the population of Malibu nearly tripled. Residents requested local bus service along Pacific Coast Highway to Santa Monica, as Greyhound's schedules were designed for long-distance travelers. The Malibu post of the American Legion began advocating for local bus service. One member, Major Robert Hoyme, was vice-president of Mack Truck's bus division.

Christopher Robert Hoyme was born on April 11, 1888, to Reverend Gjermund and Ida Hoyme in Eau Claire, Wisconsin. In the early 1910s, he worked as a sales manager at several early automobile manufacturers, including Autocar, International Motor and Alco.

During World War I, he served in the American Expeditionary Forces in France, rising to the rank of major. After the war, Major Hoyme worked as a Madison Avenue advertising executive and then traveled to Egypt in 1922 to accompany Lord Carnavon and Howard Carter on their exploration of King Tutankhamun's tomb. After returning to the United States, Major Hoyme became manager of Mack Truck's bus division in Chicago. The company transferred him to its Los Angeles office in 1942.

Hoyme applied to the California Public Utilities Commission for the necessary certificate. Greyhound did not protest Hoyme's application, clearing the way for the local bus service.

Hoyme's bus line, dubbed "Shoreline Transit," started on August 17, 1946. Among the celebrities attending the opening ceremony were comedian Ole Olsen and actor (and unofficial Malibu "mayor") Wayne Baxter. Santa Monica mayor Ray Schafer, along with Baxter, cut a ribbon across Pacific Coast Highway, and the first bus rolled into service.

Shoreline Transit operated two routes: Santa Monica–Malibu and Santa Monica–Topanga Canyon. The company had a nautical theme. Hoyme called the buses "Shoreliners"; the drivers, sporting blue sailors' uniforms, were referred to as "skippers." The buses even had racks for fishing poles. On Sundays, special runs from Santa Monica connected with the *Lenbrook* and *Gee Bee* fishing boats.

Unfortunately, low ridership and mechanical problems bedeviled Shoreline Transit. The company canceled the Topanga Canyon route in 1947 and suspended operations during the winter in 1950. After Major Hoyme died on October 20, 1950, Henry Turcotte and Harold Van Wagner, two Shoreline Transit skippers, acquired the company in February 1951. Shoreline Transit continued to lose money. About 350

Shoreline Transit opening festivities. *From left to right*: Actor Leo Carillo, Santa Monica mayor Ray Schafer and Malibu "mayor" Warner Baxter. *Courtesy Malibu Lagoon Museum.*

daily fares were needed to break even, but the buses carried only about 100 passengers each day. On December 23, 1952, the buses, festooned with banners announcing, "We did the best we could," made their final runs. The demise of Shoreline Transit left Malibu without local public transportation until 1973.

FRANK HENDLER'S "THE BUS"

Frank Hendler was born on February 12, 1929, and grew up in West Los Angeles, attending Hamilton High School and UCLA. By the mid-1960s, he had become an architect and moved to Malibu, where he designed several luxury houses. In 1970, he became the director of the Malibu Community Coordinating Committee, a citizens group designed to call attention to tasks it felt the County of Los Angeles was not performing well, as well as to give Malibu a sense of community.

Malibu residents again started requesting bus service along PCH. People were spending a lot of time driving their children to and from the beach, school and other activities. Traffic speeds and the lack of sidewalks made walking or biking dangerous. Buses would also give visitors an alternative to driving to the beach, reducing the number of cars on PCH and the need for beachfront parking.

Although a local bar owner collected one thousand signatures on a petition requesting Santa Monica Municipal Bus Lines to extend service from Santa Monica to Malibu, Jack Hutchinson, the bus line's director, expressed skepticism about ridership. He was also concerned that the frequent traffic jams on PCH would make it difficult to keep the buses on schedule.

Santa Monica's lack of interest only made the Committee more determined to provide bus service. Under the direction of Hendler, the Committee contracted with a local charter bus company to serve PCH between Santa Monica and Malibu. The buses were equipped with tape players and could carry surfboards, fishing poles and other beach gear.

The Malibu Recreational Transit System, or "The Bus," made its first run on June 16, 1973. One route ran from the Malibu Civic Center to Santa Monica and the other from the Civic Center to Trancas Beach. An all-day ticket cost fifty cents. Young people headed to the beach made up most of the riders; senior citizens also enjoyed the mobility provided by the new line. "The Bus" carried between 350 and 450 riders each weekday and 250 on Saturdays. No service operated on Sunday.

Hendler's new bus service raised eyebrows at the California Public Utilities Commission when officials found out that he had started the service without applying for the required certificate. Upon notification, Hendler quickly submitted the proper forms, and the buses kept rolling.

In order to break even, 2,600 passengers per week would have to ride. Since weekly ridership was only 2,000, Hendler expected community donations to make up the shortfall. But many pledged donations were never received. Hendler paid the difference out of his own pocket and warned that the service would shut down if the money never came in.

"People told us they would donate to us tomorrow," he said. "Well, tomorrow is here and there's not enough money left to run the bus today." Hendler vowed to keep the service running until the Southern California Rapid Transit District (RTD) started its Valley–Santa Monica bus later that summer, hoping that RTD passengers arriving in Santa Monica would boost ridership by transferring to "The Bus."

After service ended for the season on September 7, Hendler discovered that "The Bus" had nearly broken even. Encouraged by several phone calls urging him to keep the buses running, Hendler announced plans to restart the service next year, continue operating it throughout the year and add routes to UCLA and Pepperdine University, which had moved to Malibu in 1972. He negotiated with the Santa Monica Municipal Bus Lines to provide a bus at a reduced rate.

Hendler applied to the Urban Mass Transportation Administration to obtain federal funding for his bus system. But UMTA focused on helping big-city transit systems. After being turned down by the agency, Hendler proposed a "community transportation improvement district" that would tax Malibu residents to provide funding for the bus system.

Although Los Angeles mayor Tom Bradley expressed a mild interest in Hendler's community bus system, officials of the County of Los Angeles were more interested in extending RTD bus service to Malibu. The county had subsidized an RTD shuttle bus along the coast between Malibu and Manhattan Beach during the same summer Hendler was operating "The Bus."

In May 1974, the county approved RTD Line #175 between Santa Monica and Trancas Canyon on a six-month trial. Unlike "The Bus," RTD had no provision for carrying bikes or surfboards. After the trial, Hendler, with Hutchinson now in agreement, asked that the Santa Monica Municipal Bus Lines be allowed to take over the Malibu route, as its costs were lower than those of RTD. But the Los Angeles County Board of Supervisors wanted RTD to run the bus route, and RTD insisted on keeping it. RTD (and its successor, Metro) has operated bus service along Pacific Coast Highway to the present date.

PARKS AND POLITICS

In addition to his community-organizing activities, Hendler was a vocal proponent of preserving open space in the Santa Monica Mountains. "You can't compare these mountains with Big Sur or Yosemite," he said. "But they're the best we have, and there are 10 million people living in the Los Angeles area. Those mountains are a very beautiful thing, but you have to feel that by hiking right into them," he said. After the National Park Service formed the Santa Monica Mountains National Recreation Area in 1978, Hendler joined the Santa Monica Mountains Trails Council and continued to advocate for improving the park.

Hendler was also in favor of cityhood for Malibu. During the spring of 1976, he campaigned in favor of a cityhood ballot measure and ran for one of the city council seats that would be available if cityhood were approved. When the bid failed, Hendler, along with the four other candidates receiving the most votes, formed a "Cityless Council."

After a few years in Santa Fe, New Mexico, Hendler moved to Pietra Santa, Italy. There, he designed two identical marble sculptures, named *The Peacemakers*, commemorating the historic December 7, 1987 meeting between U.S. president Ronald Reagan and Soviet general secretary Mikhail Gorbachev. Sadly, he did not live to see the final placement of *The Peacemakers*, as he passed away on October 15, 1989. In the early 1990s, the artworks were installed at Shenandoah University in Virginia and at the Federation of Peace and Conciliation in Moscow.

Epilogue

Frank Hendler's dream came true on March 28, 1991, when Malibu became an incorporated city. The days of the gates and the armed riders guarding the Rindges' ranch were seemingly over. However, Malibu remains somewhat isolated, both socially and geographically. Other than PCH, road access is limited to several winding mountain roads.

In Malibu, the average home costs in the tens of millions of dollars. Residents, many of whom are celebrities or business moguls, have made it difficult for the general public to access beaches near their properties, even though the beach below the mean high tide line is legally available to all. The Colony remains a very exclusive neighborhood in Malibu, inhabited by today's stars and gated for privacy.

Most people who can afford to live in Malibu do not ride the bus. Metro Route #534 transports mostly domestic employees and a few beachgoers from Greater Los Angeles. After about seventy-five years of service, Greyhound discontinued its route through Malibu in April 2005 because of low ridership.

While Metro's #534 and a Los Angeles County summer-only "Beach Bus" through Topanga Canyon are not the modern-day descendants of Francis Brunner's Topanga and Las Flores Canyon Stages, these bus routes allow anyone to enjoy a trip along the coast, seeing it as Brunner saw it, where the only "blues" are "blues of rollicking ocean waves, the blues of clearest skies, and the blues of range on range of distant mountains."

CHAPTER 7

BUSES RUN IN THIS FAMILY

The Carsons

Mention the name Carson to a Southern Californian, and the city of Carson most likely comes to mind. That city is named after John Manuel Carson, son of George Henry Carson and Maria Victoria Dominguez. The Dominguezes were the owners of the forty-eight-thousand-acre Rancho San Pedro. Part of this Spanish land grant, which covered most of southern Los Angeles County, became the city of Carson in 1968.

However, much of the public transit history of this area rests with another, unrelated Carson family. Dean Carson came to Southern California after World War I and founded a local bus line in 1945; this simple operation grew into a transit company spanning nearly all of southern Los Angeles County, plus parts of Orange County. His descendants own and operate several bus-related industries to this day.

DEAN CARSON

Dean Carson was born on October 31, 1895, in the town of Washburn, Wisconsin. When he became old enough, Dean worked on the family farm until 1918, when he was called to serve in World War I. After the war, Dean settled in Los Angeles and then relocated to Lynwood, a predominately agricultural suburb fifteen miles southeast of downtown Los Angeles. In

Lynwood, he owned a heavy equipment rental company and a sign painting business.

Dean married Carrie Swanby and had several children, including Nadeane (born in January 1926), David (born in August 1927) and James (born in April 1930).

DEAN ENTERS THE BUS BUSINESS

Public transit in Lynwood was limited to a Pacific Electric rail line between Los Angeles and Santa Ana via Watts, as well as a Pacific Electric bus line along Long Beach Boulevard linking Huntington Park and Long Beach.

In 1943, Dean Carson, encouraged by his son David and City Councilman Cliff Schorck, applied for and was granted a twenty-five-year franchise to operate a bus route within Lynwood. However, during World War II, buses

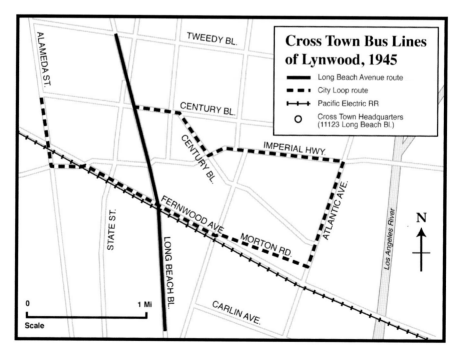

Cross Town Bus Lines, Lynwood, 1945. *Author's collection/Mapcraft.*

were severely rationed. It was not until November 1945 that the Carsons were able to obtain their first two buses.

Nearly all members of the family drove: Dean, David, James and Nadeane (female bus drivers were rare, although many drove during the war). David left Cross Town in 1952 to become vice-president of sales at Crown Coach, a major manufacturer of buses.

When the Carsons started expanding service outside Lynwood, they needed to apply to the California Public Utilities Commission (CPUC) for the necessary certificate.

CPUC let Cross Town expand where there was no existing transit service: westward on Imperial Highway to Hawthorne and southward to Compton. However, when the Carsons applied for a bus line from Lynwood to Huntington Park, the Los Angeles Transit Lines protested. LATL already ran a bus between Huntington Park and Lynwood and did not welcome competition. In September 1949, CPUC sided with LATL and rejected Cross Town's application.

Dean was livid. "There is no hope for expansion of my line under the present setup in the PUC," he said. "It's impossible to get a fair shake with them. The PE and the LATL are too big for me to buck by myself and in spite of the fact that the two big companies are set up to get 30 cents from anyone wanting to get anywhere, I have been unable to get approval for a cheaper service."

Nadeane's Polka Dot Buses

After CPUC rejected Cross Town's extension to Huntington Park, Nadeane approached the Huntington Park City Council with a plan to operate a local bus service entirely within the city; CPUC permission would not be required. The council, although supportive of the idea, was concerned that the city might have to subsidize the bus service. But after LATL raised fares on its local bus route through Huntington Park in December 1950, the council voted to support Nadeane's bus line. Service began on December 18, in the middle of the Christmas shopping season.

Cross Town Lines of Huntington Park was a separate company from the rest of the Cross Town/Southern Cities route network. Nadeane owned and managed the company and even drove a bus occasionally.

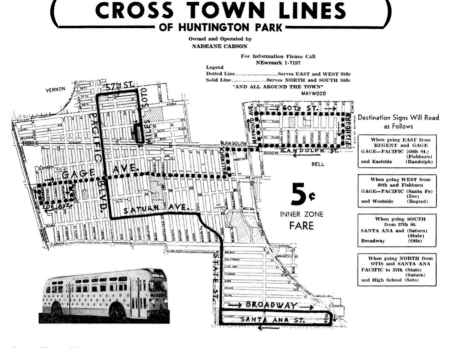

Cross Town Huntington Park schedule. *Courtesy Dorothy Peyton Gray Transportation Library.*

The buses sported a whimsical "polka dot" theme, and the drivers wore polka-dot ties.

The Carsons operated similar one-city services in Fullerton, Norwalk and Downey. The Fullerton route was expanded to Anaheim, but the Norwalk and Downey services lasted only one or two years.

CHARTERS AND CAMPFIRE GIRLS

Cross Town Bus Lines also provided charter bus service. Most of Cross Town's charter business involved transporting youth groups to campsites.

Before 1963, CPUC did not regulate charter buses, but local jurisdictions did. In 1950, Los Angeles authorized six charter bus companies to do business within the city. Cross Town Bus Lines applied for a license but was turned down.

However, Cross Town had already entered into an agreement to take a group of Campfire Girls to a mountain camp. On July 20, 1950, Dean, James and another driver arrived at the appointed place and time. They loaded the girls onto the buses and had just started on the trip when the city transportation inspector and the police showed up. They unloaded the buses and left the bewildered girls sitting on the sidewalk, while Dean and the other drivers were taken off to jail. The trip organizers hurriedly arranged transportation with one of the city's "approved" charter bus companies. The trip finally left—three hours late and in the heat of the day.

The press directed outrage at the city for its handling of the situation. "Inexcusable Stupidity of Officialdom" thundered a *Herald-Express* newspaper editorial, while the *Los Angeles Times* printed pictures of tearful girls and bus drivers being arrested.

The City of Los Angeles eventually granted Cross Town permission to operate charter bus service within Los Angeles.

ACQUISITION AND EXPANSION

Barred from expanding northward into LATL territory, Dean turned his attention to several small bus operators in the southern part of Los Angeles County. Many of these bus companies had financial difficulties, and Dean thought that acquiring and consolidating them into one larger operation would be more efficient. CPUC, apparently in agreement, granted permission for most of Dean's acquisitions.

Dean first acquired Southern Cities Transit, which operated in and around Compton. Since 1945, SCT had been owned by the Crown Coach Company. Not finding the system profitable enough, Crown sold SCT to the Carsons in April 1954. Next on Dean's list was the Holbrook–Benton Bus Line in December 1954. This company served the cities of Huntington Park, Bell, Whittier, Norwalk, Artesia and Bellflower. Another Crown-owned system, Whittier Bus Lines, was acquired in 1957.

In 1958, Dean acquired Sunset Stages, a transit system operating in Inglewood and the three beach cities (Redondo, Manhattan and Hermosa). Under Carson ownership, service on Hawthorne Boulevard between Inglewood and Torrance was improved to run every ten minutes, a rarity outside Los Angeles proper.

Governmental subsidies for public transit were nonexistent, so each segment of every route had to justify its existence by generating fare revenue. Dean continued to adjust bus routes in all of his systems, adding a portion of a route here, deleting a route segment there and rerouting yet another route elsewhere. He made route changes so quickly that he sometimes failed to file them with CPUC, or did so after the fact. Although CPUC could have fined or otherwise sanctioned Dean, the Commission's concern about the financial status of these bus lines usually meant that he was simply admonished to file the proper paperwork next time.

Dean acquired his last bus company in 1959. The Southland Bus Company, owned by William Bourne, operated between Long Beach and Anaheim, serving Disneyland and Knotts Berry Farm.

UNIONS AND STRIKES

The increasing cost of wages paid to drivers, mechanics and other employees affected Dean's bus companies. Employees unionized and demanded higher wages. To meet the higher labor costs, Dean's choices were: cutting back service; raising fares, if CPUC gave permission; or refusing to give in to the employees' demands, risking a strike.

In July 1953, the drivers and mechanics of Southern Cities Lines, at the time controlled but not fully owned by Dean, went on strike for a wage increase. At the end of the strike, the employees got their raise, and fares were raised from fifteen to twenty cents.

Another strike took place in October 1954, after Dean had acquired the Benton–Holbrook routes. This two-month-long strike turned violent when gunshots, fired from a passing car, struck two buses at the depot. Fortunately, no one was hurt.

Dean's treatment of his employees landed him in court at least twice. In 1955, a judge ordered him to pay back wages withheld during one of the strikes.

CONSOLIDATION

Although Dean had attempted to consolidate his bus companies into one large operation in 1954, both he and the CPUC subsequently decided that

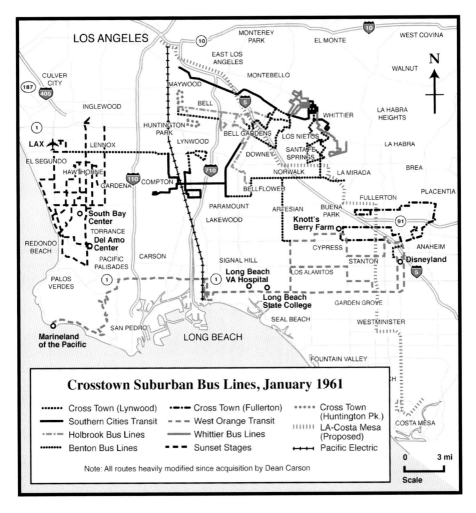

Cross Town Suburban Bus Lines, 1961. *Author's collection/Mapcraft.*

it was not quite the right time to do so. But in late 1959, the CPUC finally allowed Dean to consolidate his bus companies. The original Lynwood Cross Town Bus Lines, Southern Cities Transit, the Holbrook–Benton Bus Lines and Southland Bus Lines were all merged into a new company called Cross Town Suburban Bus Lines. The local services in Fullerton, Downey and Huntington Park were not included in the consolidation but remained separate entities owned by various Carson family members.

AT THE END OF THE ROAD

By 1960, Cross Town Suburban Bus Lines was operating eighty-four buses on twenty-two routes, covering roughly 720 square miles. But consolidation was not sufficient to make the transit system profitable. Cross Town's service area was still mostly rural. New housing developments built were low density and not conducive to high public transit use. Besides, most of the people moving to the area already owned or planned to purchase automobiles.

Dean proposed a new express route between Costa Mesa and downtown Los Angeles, the first ever Cross Town bus route to enter the central city. But LAMTA, which operated express bus service along the Santa Ana Freeway, opposed Cross Town's application. The Los Angeles Board of Public Utilities and Transportation also opposed the new route because Cross Town had not arranged for an off-street layover area in downtown Los Angeles. CPUC rejected Dean's application.

Hassles with various government agencies, financial difficulties in obtaining new buses and his own personal health problems convinced Dean to retire from the transit business. In January 1961, Dean sold the Cross Town Suburban Lines, plus the Fullerton and Huntington Park operations, to LAMTA for $346,093. By February 15, LAMTA buses were rolling where

Cross Town Suburban Bus Lines. *Courtesy Dorothy Peyton Gray Transportation Library.*

Cross Town buses once did. Many of the Cross Town drivers and mechanics became LAMTA employees.

CARSONS: THE SECOND GENERATION

While Dean enjoyed his sunset years, his two sons, David and James, continued in the bus business.

In 1962, shortly after Cross Town was sold, David left Crown Coach and founded the American International Bus Exchange. AIBE acted as a broker between transit companies wishing to sell older buses and bus operators seeking to save money by buying used equipment. David facilitated the sale of the last of LAMTA's streetcars to Cairo, Egypt, and its electric trolleybuses to Mexico City. David's three sons—Dean, Dwight and Dale—helped in the family business with tasks ranging from repairing and maintaining buses to selling them.

David sold AIBE to the American Chromalloy Company in 1977. The company renamed AIBE to Hausman Bus Sales. David retired shortly thereafter, although his sons Dean and Dale stayed with the new company.

After the Cross Town sale, James worked at LAMTA (which became the Southern California Rapid Transit District in 1964) as a division manager. In 1971, he moved to San Diego Transit to become that agency's assistant manager. One year later, James relocated to Hawaii and became assistant manager of Honolulu Transit ("The Bus"). By 1972, he had become president of Hawaiian Scenic Tours.

In 1975, James returned to the mainland to head the Western Division of ARA Services, owner of Hawaiian Scenic. ARA, located in Encino, operated school and charter buses. Its vehicles provided athlete transportation during the 1984 Los Angeles Olympics. Shortly after the Games, Laidlaw Transit of Toronto, Canada, acquired ARA's bus operations; James retired about a month later.

COMMUTER BUS LINES

Douglas Bus Lines (DBL) was a commuter buspool service dating from the years after World War II, when it carried employees to the Douglas Aircraft plant in Long Beach. Later, DBL expanded to serve other businesses. DBL's motley fleet of former RTD and Greyhound buses constantly had mechanical and safety problems, often getting the firm in trouble with CPUC.

In 1977, James and former Cross Town employee William Bourne purchased DBL. Since the bus line no longer exclusively served Douglas facilities, they renamed it Commuter Bus Lines (CBL). They disposed of the worst of the secondhand vehicles and expanded service. James managed the existing Southern California operations, while William, formerly the manager of the Sacramento Regional Transit System, set up a route network serving the Sacramento metropolitan area.

In addition to its home-to-work commuter buspool service, CBL offered charter service, racetrack specials to Santa Anita and Hollywood Park, a "gamblers special" from Sacramento to Reno, airport buses to the Sacramento Airport and a shuttle bus serving California state offices. CBL also operated Yolobus, a local transit system between Sacramento and Yolo County.

INNOVATIONS IN COMMUTING

Traditionally, commuter buspools, including CBL's, carried only employees of a single employer. For example, if the bus was going to the Rockwell plant in El Segundo, it would not accept passengers working for a different company, even if that company was next door. CBL considered that practice to be inefficient. It claimed that if it could carry anyone to El Segundo on any bus, regardless of employer, then more of its buses would run full and its operation would be much more efficient in terms of both vehicle and energy usage.

CBL proposed its buspool routes be allowed to carry anyone wanting to travel to any employer in what was called the "LAX–El Segundo Employment Area." Competing buspool operators objected, citing employer concerns about confidentiality and corporate espionage. In 1983, CPUC sided with CBL, agreeing that dedicated buses restricted to employees of one employer was unreasonable.

Insurance Troubles and Sale to Kirkman

In December 1985, Transit Casualty, CBL's insurance carrier, abruptly went out of business. CPUC immediately suspended CBL's certificate due to lack of insurance. CBL's operations in Southern California and in Sacramento were pulled off the street. Replacement insurance would cost nearly four times as much as the Transit Casualty coverage.

T.R. Kirkman, who owned stock in the Pacific Trailways bus system, bought CBL from Bourne and Carson in March 1986. Because of his partial ownership of Pacific Trailways, Kirkman was able to obtain insurance at a much lower rate. Under Kirkman, CBL added new routes from Orange County and the San Fernando Valley to downtown Los Angeles.

Dale Carson, son of David Carson, had been the general manager of CBL since March 1986. In December, Kirkman sold the Southern California division to Dale and his sister, Dawn, while retaining the Sacramento-based services.

Lynwood Trolley

In mid-1986, Lynwood city officials decided to provide a local shuttle bus to supplement the service provided by RTD. A half-cent sales tax provided funds for cities to set up local transit systems within their borders.

The city bought two red "rubber-tired trolleys" (small buses designed to resemble streetcars) and contracted with Commuter Bus Lines to operate them on a route looping around the city. CBL stored and maintained the trolleys at its yard at 11123 Long Beach Boulevard—the same yard where Dean Carson had started Cross Town Bus Lines nearly forty years earlier.

The Lynwood Trolley started service in late December. The trolleys charged no fare, and by late February, ridership was about fifteen thousand per month. Senior citizens and the handicapped enjoyed their newfound mobility, while the younger set used the trolleys to get home from after-school activities.

The Lynwood Trolley added two new routes in 1990. A fourth line connecting downtown Lynwood to the Metro Blue Line was added in 1992. The free ride lasted until 1994, when a twenty-five-cent fare went into effect.

Lynwood Trolley. *Author's collection.*

In 2000, Paul Richards, a former mayor of Lynwood, abused his authority by forcing Commuter Bus Lines, and other companies with city contracts, to pay for consulting services provided by a company owned by Richards's family. CBL was never implicated in any wrongdoing. However, all city contracts were rescinded in 2003, and another contractor was selected to operate the Lynwood Trolley.

The Lynwood Trolley was the last of the Carson bus operations. As other private bus operators entered the field, the Carsons focused on maintaining, selling and leasing transit vehicles rather than providing bus service. During the late 1980s and early '90s, Commuter Bus Lines obtained contracts with the Orange County Transit District, the University of California–Los Angeles and other entities to maintain and refurbish buses.

THE CARSON LEGACY CONTINUES

Dean and Dale Carson started several companies during the late 1980s, all dedicated to the sale, repair, refurbishment or leasing of buses and intercity coaches. Complete Coach Works refurbishes and upgrades used buses, and

Shuttle Bus Leasing offers temporary rental of buses (for airport shuttles and the Olympic Games). Transit Sales International buys used buses from transit agencies and then refurbishes and resells them. TSI has had much success selling buses on the international market, ranging from Canada, Mexico and Central America to China and the Philippines.

Dean's sons, David and Kyle, as well as Dale's sons, Bradley, Elliot and Kris, participated in the family businesses as soon as they were old enough. They are all currently employed in one of the Carson companies.

EPILOGUE

LAMTA and its successor agencies (RTD, MTA/Metro) have operated the former Cross Town bus routes since their acquisition in 1961; service in Orange County was transferred to the Orange County Transit District in the mid-'70s. The transit agencies have renumbered, restructured and rerouted these lines so often it can be difficult to trace the former Cross Town bus routes.

The cities of Downey, Norwalk and Huntington Park, once served by Carson family–owned bus companies, all have their own municipal bus lines. Also still operating is the Lynwood Trolley, the resurrection of Dean Carson's original local line, but with a different contractor and a new name—Lynwood Breeze. The former Cross Town Bus/Lynwood Trolley yard at 11123 Long Beach Boulevard was sold to an adjacent shopping center.

In 2010, Complete Coach Works opened a plant in Puerto Rico to refurbish buses owned by the Metropolitan Bus Authority in San Juan. Bradley Carson manages the forty-thousand-square-foot facility, capable of rehabbing seventeen buses at once.

Bradley, along with his siblings and cousins, represents the fourth generation of Carsons in the bus business. If the past is a predictor of the future, then it is certain that their children, and maybe their grandchildren, will keep the family businesses going and continue the legacy started by a sign painter in Lynwood back in 1943.

CHAPTER 8

THE SCHOOL BUS SCANDAL

The Landiers

The Landiers of San Pedro were another family who influenced Southern California's transportation history. Felicien Landier, along with his two sons, Felicien Paul ("F.P.") and Robert, turned a group of undisciplined jitney drivers into the San Pedro Motor Bus Company. F.P. also improved bus service in Watts and, during the 1940s and '50s, operated a large fleet of buses for the Los Angeles City Schools. However, a California Grand Jury investigation of the school system unearthed a conflict of interest scandal that not only put F.P. out of the school bus business but also laid bare his convoluted marital life.

NEW ORLEANS

Felicien Landier, the son of French immigrants Julien and Felicite Landier, was born in New Orleans on June 14, 1879. When Felicien was a young child, the family returned to France. He attended school in Paris and excelled in music. The Landiers returned to New Orleans in 1887, and Felicien, as he grew older, played in the New Orleans orchestra.

LA BOURGOGNE AND THE SPANISH-AMERICAN WAR

The Landiers, either separately or together, traveled back and forth between France and the United States on the fast steamships of the Compagnie Generale Transatlantique, or French Line. These ships crossed the Atlantic in seven days. However, the French Line was often accused of operating its ships recklessly.

On July 3, 1898, Julien boarded the French ship *La Bourgogne* in New York for a trip to France. As the ship traversed the North Atlantic, it encountered a heavy fog. In the early morning of July 4, *La Bourgogne* collided with an English ship, *Cromartyshire*, near Cape Sable, Nova Scotia.

The scene aboard the French ship was one of chaos and desperation. Crew members used fists and knives to push passengers out of lifeboats to save themselves. Although nearly half of the 220 crew members were saved, just 70 of the 506 passengers survived, including only one woman and no children. Julien, a third-class passenger, did not survive.

At the time *La Bourgogne* sank, Felicite and two other children were in France and decided to remain there. Felicien enlisted with the Naval Reserves and served as a bugler in the Spanish-American War.

La Bourgogne at Le Havre, France. *Photochrom Prints Collection, Library of Congress.*

In December 1898, Felicien married Alice Delormel. Over the next eight years, Felicien and Alice had four children, including Felicien Paul ("F.P.") and Robert.

San Pedro Motor Bus Association

In 1909, the Landiers moved to Los Angeles, where Felicien found work as a bandleader, a laundryman and a jitney driver. The Landiers settled in San Pedro in 1915. Felicien started several businesses, including a bowling alley (he was an avid bowler), a candy shop and a soft drink bottling company. He also served as an agent for the French ships calling at San Pedro. Felicien was extremely civic-minded; one of his projects was developing the land at Point Fermin into a public park.

Along with Pacific Electric's local streetcars, jitney buses, predominately driven by Italian immigrants, provided public transportation in San Pedro. Seventh Street and Harbor Avenue was the "hub," where buses departed and returned. The Landiers managed two routes: one to Point Fermin and another to White Point. Other routes in San Pedro were "owned" by individual families. The Bono family operated the Barton Hill bus route, while the La Rambla neighborhood was covered by the La Pinta family.

Drawing on his experience as a jitney driver, Felicien organized the drivers into the San Pedro Motor Bus Association. Drivers joined by providing a bus and agreeing to follow established routes, maintain schedules and operate in an orderly fashion. Managing all of these independent drivers was not easy. Each driver was out for himself, and drivers cutting in front of one another in competition for fares was common. Arguments and even fistfights between drivers happened often. Felicien would request that the Los Angeles Board of Public Utilities and Transportation revoke the permit of a particularly disagreeable or insubordinate driver.

F.P. and his younger brother, Robert, entered the bus business as soon as they were old enough. F.P. became a driver and a mechanic, while Robert, who also owned an insurance agency, managed two of the San Pedro bus lines.

During the Great Depression and into World War II, the buses were profitable, as relatively few San Pedrans owned automobiles. Employees of the tuna canneries on Terminal Island rode the bus to the ferry terminal

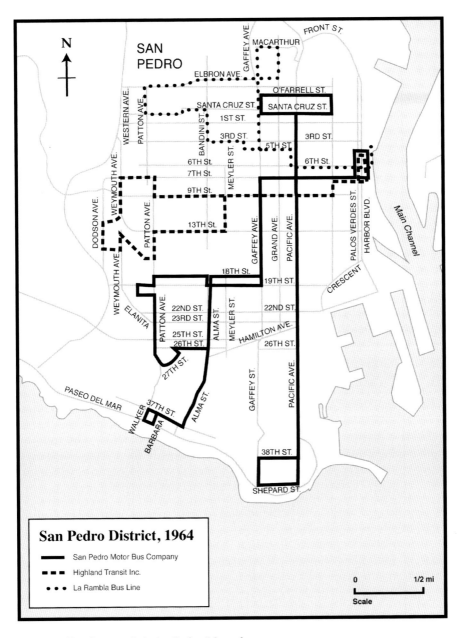

San Pedro Bus System. *Author's collection/Mapcraft.*

and then boarded the ferry to their jobs. Soldiers and sailors from Fort MacArthur and the Pacific Fleet were frequent bus users. The buses were so popular that Pacific Electric abandoned its local San Pedro streetcars in 1938, leaving only the interurbans to Los Angeles and Long Beach. In 1943, the association became the San Pedro Motor Bus Corporation.

Robert continued managing the bus system until 1971. Faced with aging buses, rising labor and insurance costs and increased use of private automobiles, the bus company went out of business, and the Southern California Rapid Transit District (RTD) took over the routes.

THE LANDIERS TAKE OVER BUSES IN WATTS

In the early 1920s, Felicien and F.P. decided to expand their transportation business to other parts of Southern California. In 1926, they turned their attention to Watts, a small city that became a part of Los Angeles on May 28.

Watts, originally a small agricultural settlement near a Pacific Electric railway junction, became an incorporated city in 1907. The first African Americans to settle in Watts were railway workers. More arrived from the South during World War I seeking employment and a better life. A substantial Mexican American population lived there too. Most businesses in Watts, however, were owned or controlled by whites.

Local entrepreneurs used horse-drawn carriages to take people to and from the Pacific Electric stations in and near Watts. In the 1910s, they started using automobiles, and then small buses, for this purpose. It was easy to get a bus franchise in Watts; often a hastily scrawled note to the city trustees was all that was necessary. By the early 1920s, an informal network of owner-operator driven routes had developed.

After annexation, officials from Los Angeles's BPU&T sent an inspector to Watts to investigate the bus services. The inspector's report described buses operating on irregular schedules, drivers failing to complete trips and bus runs canceled if a more profitable charter bus request came along. When the BPU&T tried to enforce minimum standards in 1927, there was much opposition. One driver had his permit revoked for making death threats against the inspector. Certain other drivers offered to sell their permits and vehicles.

The Landiers began acquiring the permits of the independent operators and consolidating the routes under a single company. Because most bus

Left: F.P. Landier.
*Los Angeles Public
Library Photo
Collection.*

Below: General
Motors school bus
advertisement.
Author's collection.

31 GENERAL MOTORS BUSES

**.... Carry School Children
Safely and on Schedule**

SAFETY and DEPENDABILITY are of vital importance in a School Bus—so Kemble & Landier, school bus contractors in the Los Angeles District—operate thirty-one GMC'S. These units carry precious cargoes safely and on time. ● Upkeep is exceedingly low – quality of performance is exceedingly high. ● GENERAL MOTORS equipment will solve *your* hauling problem, too. Whether you need Trucks,

Buses or Trailers, there's a GMC to more than meet your requirements. Learn about them – *Now!*

GENERAL MOTORS' TRUCK CO., 1850 E. WASHINGTON BLVD., LOS ANGELES
TIME PAYMENTS AVAILABLE THROUGH OUR OWN Y.M.A.C.

GENERAL MOTORS TRUCKS & TRAILERS

owner-operators were African American, members of the black community, led by Walter R. Knox, protested the Landier takeover. Knox accused the BPU&T and the chamber of commerce of driving the owner-operators out of business and giving the permits to the white Landiers. BPU&T officials tried to assure the community that its decision was based on service quality, not on race. However, Knox, along with other black citizens in Watts, remained unconvinced.

By October 1928, the Landiers, operating as L&L Transportation Company, had acquired all local bus services in and around Watts. In 1936, F.P. bought out his father's interest in L&L and formed a partnership with William C. Kemble. The new company operated transit and school buses under the name Landier and Kemble. After two years, Kemble sold his share of the business to F.P., who then formed a new company, Landier Transit.

Gardena and Torrance

In 1939, Pacific Electric, facing financial difficulties, announced the cancelation of several routes, including the route serving Gardena and Torrance. PE planned to replace several rail lines with buses, but not the Gardena–Torrance route, leaving the two cities to develop their own bus service.

The last PE train clattered through Gardena during the night of January 14, 1940. The next morning, Landier Transit buses, under contract to Gardena, operated along a route connecting the city with Los Angeles Railway's streetcar terminal at Vermont Avenue and 116th Street. Simultaneously, the City of Torrance started a bus line that provided direct, no-transfer-needed service to downtown Los Angeles. Asbury Rapid Transit System, which primarily served the San Fernando Valley, operated the Torrance–Los Angeles bus route.

Officials of both Gardena and Torrance hoped that either Landier or Asbury would operate the bus service as a profit-making concern. Landier proposed a route serving Torrance, Gardena, Watts and Huntington Park. Passengers going to Los Angeles could transfer to either the Los Angeles Railway streetcar or the Pacific Electric. The proposed Asbury route would connect Walteria, Lomita, Torrance, Gardena and downtown Los Angeles.

Because the Railroad Commission was unlikely to approve both routes, each company, with its respective city behind it, promoted its route as the best

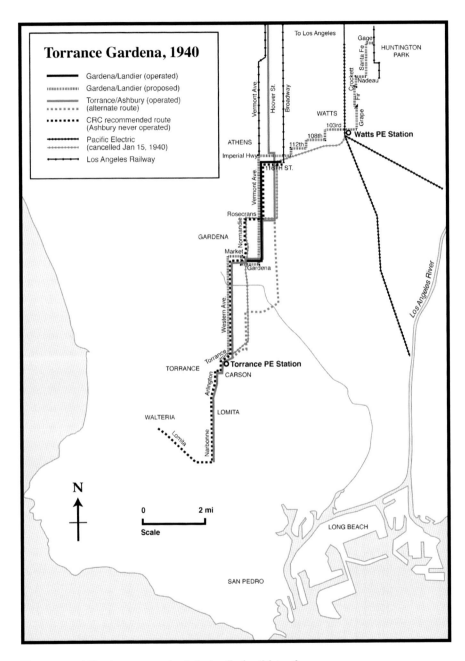

Torrance and Gardena proposals. *Author's collection/Mapcraft.*

choice. The debate between the two proposals raged in both city councils and in the press. The *Torrance Herald* supported the Asbury plan, while the *Gardena Valley News* endorsed Landier's offering.

Torrance mayor William H. Tolson, on discussing the Landier route, said, "We don't want anything to do with that kind of a deal. In the first place, our residents want transportation to and from Los Angeles, not Huntington Park or Watts. In the second place, such a deal would deprive Walteria and Lomita residents of through bus service they now enjoy with the Torrance municipal buses."

Los Angeles's BPU&T opposed the Asbury route because the company planned to allow local passengers to ride between Imperial Highway and downtown Los Angeles, taking business away from the streetcars.

On June 18, 1940, the Commission rejected the Landier proposal and granted Asbury a certificate to provide bus service from Torrance and Gardena to the 116th Street/Vermont streetcar terminal. No service to downtown Los Angeles or Walteria would be provided. Unhappy with the Commission's decision, the two cities decided to continue operating their municipal buses. Torrance Transit and Gardena Municipal Bus Lines have operated ever since.

F.P. still insisted that a bus to Huntington Park was necessary because of industrial growth in South Los Angeles. He applied again to the Commission. New commissioners had been appointed in the interim, and this time, the certificate was granted. On November 27, 1941, the first Landier Transit buses rolled along Pacific Boulevard in the heart of Huntington Park's shopping district.

LANDIER TRANSIT IN WARTIME

F.P. anticipated increased ridership on the Huntington Park route during the Christmas shopping season. However, the events of December 7, 1941, quickly changed everyone's priorities.

Public transportation companies across Southern California, from the vast Pacific Electric to the tiny, three-bus Victory Transit Company in Pomona, added as much service as possible to accommodate soldiers going to the battlefronts and war workers commuting to shipyards and aircraft plants. Gasoline and tires were rationed, motivating many to carpool or use public transportation.

Landier Transit added several bus routes to the shipyards on Terminal Island. Unfortunately, ridership was disappointingly low. Shipyard workers received a larger gasoline ration than ordinary commuters, encouraging them to drive to work. After a few weeks, Landier Transit discontinued the special wartime routes.

Trouble in Watts

In addition to his school and transit bus service, F.P. offered special bus routes to the Santa Anita and Hollywood Park horse racing tracks. Landier Transit acquired a certificate in 1946 to carry youth groups to Big Pines in the San Bernardino Mountains. But the groups soon decided to make other transportation arrangements, so the Big Pines route lasted only a year.

Even though the population of Watts had ballooned during and after World War II, Landier Transit had not substantially increased the level of service on its local Watts bus routes since 1930. Since most Watts residents were transit-dependent, the Watts bus routes became overwhelmed. Passengers and community leaders complained bitterly about overcrowded buses, infrequent service, disrespectful and unsafe drivers and bus stops without shelters, exposing passengers to the weather.

In early 1947, a newly formed Watts Citizens' Welfare Committee attempted to make Landier Transit aware of bus service deficiencies. On November 12, about five hundred people crowded into a BPU&T meeting. Landier Transit representatives were soundly booed when they attempted to defend the service provided.

The crowd was much more supportive of a bus system proposed by physician Dr. Simon Jaime and real estate agent Samuel Taylor, both African Americans and well regarded by the community. Their Watts Rapid Transit System had routes providing direct service to housing projects and other areas poorly served, or unserved, by Landier Transit. But what attracted the most attention was a drawing of a new terminal building for the Watts Rapid Transit buses. As the existing Pacific Electric station in Watts had fallen into disrepair, the citizens looked forward to a modern, up-to-date transit facility.

Since the proposed Watts Rapid Transit routes overlapped Landier Transit's routes, Watts Rapid Transit would be prohibited, under Commission rules, from picking up and dropping off passengers along

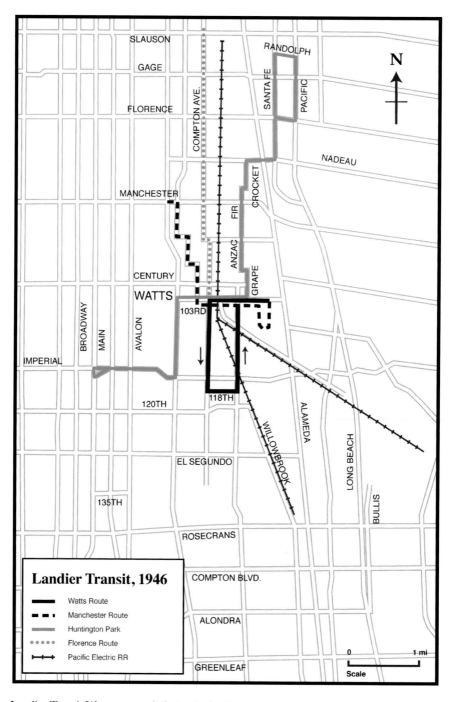

Landier Transit Watts routes. *Author's collection/Mapcraft.*

route segments also served by Landier Transit. Ben Rosenfeld, president of Landier Transit, said that Watts could not support two competing transit companies and predicted that both would go out of business if both companies were granted franchises.

The people of Watts rallied around Watts Rapid Transit. Their disdain for Landier Transit became worse after F.P. allegedly muttered a racial slur at a meeting. However, neither the BPU&T nor the Commission granted Watts Rapid Transit permission to operate, citing both competition issues and Jaime and Taylor's lack of experience in the bus business. Instead, Landier Transit was allowed to continue operating, although F.P. was warned about having a "public be damned attitude" and being "perfectly willing to give the worst service that he can get away with in the Watts District."

In response to these admonishments, F.P. improved the Watts service in 1948. Buses ran on time, and a new route on Compton Avenue, linking Watts and the Florence district, was added.

TROUBLE IN SCHOOL

By 1948, Landier Management Company, a separate division of Landier Transit, provided 95 percent of the routes serving the Los Angeles City Schools, using a fleet of two hundred buses.

In 1951, the Los Angeles County Grand Jury, hearing rumors about irregularities in hiring practices, began an investigation of the school system. Witnesses told of rigged examinations and discrimination against African American, Asian American, Jewish and middle-aged applicants.

At one grand jury hearing, school principal Ione Swan described dangerous playground equipment, tainted meat in cafeterias and financial improprieties. When the board asked her to provide evidence of her charges, she refused and was summarily dismissed.

Mrs. Swan's accusations, however, caused the grand jury to review the school system's business practices. It discovered that two board members, Roy A. Becker and Gertrude Rounsavelle, had clear conflicts of interest. Becker was an insurance broker who had written policies for Landier Transit since 1929. Gertrude Rounsavelle's husband, Lafayette, was also an insurance broker. The two brokers, starting in 1947, both insured Landier, splitting the commission between them. Three years later, F.P.'s brother, Robert, through his insurance agency, started writing policies for the bus firm and receiving one-third of the commissions.

The grand jury was empowered to either indict or accuse Becker and Rounsavelle of violating state codes regarding conflict of interest. After being presented with the evidence, the jury could vote to convict. The consequences of conviction, if the jury chose indictment, was a $1,000 fine, five years in jail and a lifetime ban on holding public office in California. A conviction on an accusation meant that the only penalty would be removal from office for the current term.

Becker denied that he had done anything illegal, while Rounsavelle pleaded ignorance of her husband's insurance business. Eleanor B. Allen, another board member, testified that she had seen Becker's name on several insurance contracts.

On March 11, 1951, the grand jury voted to accuse both Becker and Rounsavelle of breaking the conflict of interest laws. Rounsavelle faced reelection on May 29. If she were convicted and reelected, she would have only been removed from office until her new term started in July. However, she lost the election and resigned a few days before her current term ended. Becker was put on trial, convicted and removed from office.

During Becker's trial, the grand jury accused another board member, J. Paul Elliott, of conflict of interest violations. Elliott was an attorney who also worked for Landier Transit for a $200 per month retainer fee, and he had voted on the bus contracts at the same time. At his February 1952 trial, he claimed to be working for Landier Transit, which operated the Watts bus lines, rather than Landier Management, which handled the school buses. However, a review of the relationship between the two Landier companies showed that Landier Management had a controlling interest in Landier Transit. The checks Elliott received came from both companies. On March 7, he was convicted and removed from office.

Will the Real Mrs. Landier Please Stand Up?

On October 12, 1951, the grand jury, continuing its investigations, indicted board member Olin Darby for similar activities. Darby had voted on contracts favoring a print shop and an ice cream plant, both of which were tenants on land he owned. The grand jury discovered, in the course of Darby's hearing, that F.P. had invited, at his expense, several school board members and their spouses on two trips to Yosemite in 1948. As details about the trips came to light, board member Allen suddenly resigned.

While at Yosemite, F.P.'s guests thought that the woman accompanying him was his wife; everyone remembered calling her "Mrs. Landier." But shortly after these trips were brought to public attention by the grand jury hearings, F.P.'s real wife, Honor B. Landier, announced that they had been legally separated since 1943. She then sued for divorce and an injunction preventing him from selling $1 million in marital assets. F.P. claimed that he and Honor had a "Mexican divorce" (a controversial ceremony in which both spouses need not be present) in 1935. By April 1952, the story of F.P. and his "wife" was all over the national press, even in *Time* magazine. The couple finalized their "American" (and legally binding) divorce in 1953.

Voiding the Contract

Because board members with financial interests in the school bus company voted on the Landier contract, the board voted to void it. The board also prepared to sue Landier Transit to recover the money paid

Landier Transit bus. *Courtesy Motor Bus Society.*

to the company during the years the three removed board members had voted on the contract.

School would begin on September 17, 1951; there was not enough time to open bidding, vote to select a new school bus operator and start service before then. Faced with the prospect of twelve thousand students having to find alternate transportation, the board voted on September 13 to enter an emergency forty-day rental agreement with Landier, ensuring that bus service would be provided until another company could be chosen.

The end of the school bus contract left F.P. with Landier Transit in Watts. Although F.P. had made a few improvements in the 1940s, he had focused primarily on his school bus service and never gave the transit system much attention or enthusiasm. In 1952, he offered to sell the system to Frank and Herbert Atkinson, operators of the neighboring South Los Angeles Transportation Company. The sale was finalized in 1953, and F.P. was out of the bus business.

F.P.'s Financial Problems Continue

On October 24, 1952, the district sued F.P. and Landier Transit for $1.5 million, the amount paid to the bus company during the years the contract was voted on by Becker, Rounsavelle and Elliott. Probably knowing that his days in the school bus business were over, F.P. sought a settlement with the district.

F.P. and the district agreed on a settlement on August 17, 1954. F.P. was to pay the district $264,776.86 in eight yearly installments. If he missed a payment, he would be required to pay twice the outstanding balance, plus interest.

Although F.P. made payments in 1954, 1955 and 1956, by 1957 he was in serious financial trouble. Ethel Morris, the woman who had posed as his wife on the Yosemite trips, sued him in 1956 for $164,952, claiming that she acted as his housekeeper, secretary, nurse, dietitian and "business confidant" for him. F.P. paid an undisclosed settlement to her in 1959.

F.P., having difficulty making his settlement payment for 1957, asked the school board for additional time and presented the board a list of all of his assets and liabilities. Included was the Capistran Ranch, more than eight thousand acres of rugged land near the Mendocino County town of Covelo. Although F.P. had owned the ranch for several years, the ownership was now murky. F.P. had married Rose Heiner in 1957; that marriage lasted less than a year, and during divorce proceedings, the court granted her title to the ranch. Rose transferred the title to a title company in 1961. Complicating matters even further, F.P.'s first ex-wife, Honor, held a $50,000 lien on the ranch as part of her 1953 divorce settlement.

On June 14, the school system, fearing that F.P. was trying to prevent it from being awarded the ranch as part of the settlement, obtained an injunction prohibiting F.P. or any of the other titleholders from selling the ranch. A court battle over various legal aspects of the case raged for several years until 1969, when the school system was awarded 6,188 acres as payment for the settlement.

EPILOGUE

In May 1961, a company named CL Transit bid on a contract to transport handicapped students. The board quickly discovered that CL Transit was a shell company, lacking buses, drivers or even a garage. But what made the board take notice is that the company's directors were all Landiers: F.P. was an advisor; his ex-wife, Honor, was president; and his son Paul was secretary-treasurer. Additionally, F.P. still owed part of the unpaid judgment from 1954. As the scandal of 1951 was still fresh in the board members' minds, the board voted to decline CL Transit's bid.

About a year after his failed attempt to resume providing school bus service, F.P. remarried once again and moved to Oklahoma City, where he worked in the construction industry until his death on January 3, 1968.

The Los Angeles City Schools and its successor, Los Angeles Unified School District (formed in 1961), retained ownership of the Capistran Ranch for about twenty years. Cattle grazing provided a steady source of revenue. One school official considered using the property as an educational campground, but its distance from Los Angeles, as well as its undeveloped state, made that idea impractical.

One has to work hard to find much of a trace of Landier's operations. The Los Angeles Unified School District uses a mixture of directly operated and contracted companies to operate their school buses across metropolitan Los Angeles.

The Atkinsons operated the former Landier routes until 1968, when Dr. Thomas W. Matthew, an African American neurosurgeon and civil rights activist, bought the bus lines from the Atkinsons. He operated them as one of his many programs designed to provide "self-help" to the black community. Despite the doctor's enthusiasm, financial problems shut down the bus routes in September 1971, and RTD provided replacement service from then on.

Over the years, bus service in South Central Los Angeles has been extensively modified, making it difficult to trace Landier Transit's original routes. An exception is Metro Line #254, which connects Watts and Huntington Park via many of the same streets used by the former Landier Transit route.

CHAPTER 9

HELICOPTERS OVER TRAFFIC

Clarence Belinn's Los Angeles Airways

Los Angeles, along with New York, Chicago and San Francisco, was once served by regularly scheduled helicopter service. Helicopters landed and took off in several Southern California suburbs, ferrying passengers to and from Los Angeles International Airport (LAX). A flight from San Bernardino to LAX, requiring up to two hours by car, would only take thirty minutes by helicopter.

Aviation pioneer Clarence M. Belinn, a strong proponent of helicopters, founded Los Angeles Airways (LAA) in 1944. LAA transferred passengers from the suburbs to LAX. Belinn also hoped that suburban commuters could use helicopters to go to downtown Los Angeles. However, high operating costs and two fatal accidents ended Belinn's dream in 1970.

CLARENCE M. BELINN

Clarence Mauritz Belinn was born on October 24, 1903, in the coal mining town of Lanse, Pennsylvania. Most residents—including Clarence's parents, Axel and Hannah Belinn—had immigrated to the United States from Sweden in the 1880s. Axel was a coal miner until 1916, when he opened a soda bottling plant. Clarence worked in his father's bottling plant until joining the army in 1924.

Belinn enlisted in the U.S. Army Air Corps and, in technical school, learned every aspect of aviation. He was stationed at Langley Field, Virginia, when a plane made an emergency landing in June 1925. Belinn quickly diagnosed a problem with the engine's distributor and replaced the part. Years later, he learned that the pilot had been none other than aviation pioneer Igor Sikorsky.

In 1927, Belinn was stationed at March Field near Riverside, about seventy miles east of Los Angeles. The vastness of Southern California amazed him, as he noted it took more than an hour to drive from its distant suburbs to downtown Los Angeles. He envisioned a short-haul, "feeder" airline carrying passengers from the suburbs to the city and to the airport.

After leaving the army in 1929, Belinn found work at Washington–New York Airways as a pilot and mechanic. Shortly afterward, he worked at Ludington Airlines as superintendent of ground operations. When Eastern Air Lines acquired Ludington in 1933, Belinn moved to Boston-Maine Airways, as director of maintenance and engineering.

By this time, Belinn was well known in aviation circles. He helped Amelia Earhart prepare for her around-the-world flight in 1937 by adding an elaborate fueling system to her airplane.

Belinn became vice-president of Kansas City Southern Airlines in 1938. Two years later, he became vice-president of Hawaiian Airlines. He also served as director of the air transportation division of Matson Steamship Lines, where he sought to implement scheduled flights between Hawaii and the U.S. mainland. But he was rebuffed by the U.S. Civil Air Board (CAB), which ruled against steamship lines, railroads and other transportation interests owning airlines. In any event, civilian air transport was curtailed once World War II started.

In 1944, Belinn resigned from Matson to start Los Angeles Airways (LAA), the first scheduled helicopter airline.

HELICOPTERS TO THE RESCUE

Sikorsky and others had developed early forms of the helicopter, which had seen limited use toward the end of World War II. Originally, Belinn was skeptical about the hovering aircraft. "The traveling public should not be the guinea pig," he warned, and he suggested small, fixed-wing

Airmail delivered by helicopter. *Author's collection.*

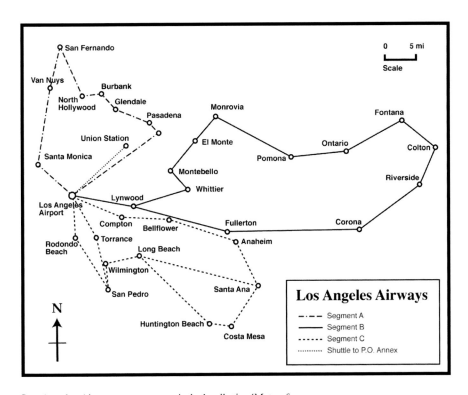

Los Angeles Airways route map. *Author's collection/Mapcraft.*

airplanes instead. But discussions with Sikorsky convinced Belinn of the advantages of helicopters. Belinn coined the terms "heliport" (a full-featured airport serving helicopters) and "helistop" (a basic heliport with limited facilities). However, further development had to wait until the war ended.

Meanwhile, the United States Post Office, which had experimented with army-operated helicopters to move the mail between airports and suburban areas since 1946, granted LAA a contract to carry mail from LAX to downtown Los Angeles and other points in Southern California.

In June 1947, the Civil Aeronautics Board (CAB) approved Belinn's application to operate his scheduled helicopter airline. Service began on October 1, using Sikorsky S-51 helicopters on a shuttle route between LAX and the Terminal Annex Post Office in downtown Los Angeles. Two other routes served the San Fernando and San Gabriel Valleys. A third route opened in 1949, serving Whittier, Long Beach and Santa Ana. The S-51 could carry ten passengers, but LAA removed most of the seats and filled the helicopters with mailbags.

Helicopter airlines started operating in Chicago in 1949 and in New York in 1953—both initially carrying mail only but adding passenger service within a few years. All three helicopter airlines had to develop methods, policies and procedures for training pilots, flying at night or in bad weather and using the radio and signaling systems.

PASSENGER SERVICE BEGINS

Belinn hesitated to carry passengers at first, as additional facilities—such as passenger waiting areas, ticket counters and baggage areas (and their associated personnel)—would be required. Therefore, although LAA was the first helicopter airline, it was not the first to carry passengers. That honor went to New York Airways in 1953.

For passenger service, LAA ordered two twelve-seat Sikorsky S-55 helicopters; these were modified to carry eight passengers and their luggage, along with the mail. Passenger service started on November 22, 1954, with six daily round trips between LAX and Long Beach. Within a year, passengers could fly to Orange County, Pomona, Riverside and San Bernardino; service reached Van Nuys in 1959. Fares varied by distance,

L.P. Doty and Clarence Belinn with a Sikorsky S-62. *Los Angeles Public Library Photo Collection.*

topping out at ten dollars for a thirty-two-minute flight from LAX to San Bernardino, LAA's longest route.

In its first year of passenger service, LAA transported 10,000 passengers. The number of passengers carried increased each year until 1967, when it peaked at 396,000. Most customers were businessmen connecting to airlines at LAX. The Anaheim heliport, near Disneyland, was the busiest, carrying about 30,000 passengers per month, many of whom were tourists. Flights on December nights, providing a fantastic view of Christmas lights from above, were popular.

HELICOPTER MASS TRANSIT

In addition to serving LAX, Belinn desired to provide helicopters for people working in downtown Los Angeles. LAA helicopters would act as

Clarence Belinn with model helicopters. *Los Angeles Public Library Photo Collection.*

flying commuter trains, shrinking commutes of over an hour by road to thirty minutes or less. But there was no passenger heliport downtown. The heliport at Terminal Annex could only accommodate small helicopters, lacked passenger facilities and was too distant from most workplaces. The Los Angeles Chamber of Commerce suggested using a parking lot near the Civic Center for a heliport.

Additionally, helicopter service was too expensive on a per-passenger basis to compete with driving or public transit. In December 1961, LAA purchased Sikorsky S61-L helicopters, each capable of carrying twenty-eight passengers. Belinn hoped that the future would bring huge, one-hundred-passenger helicopters. These large aircraft would theoretically have a per-passenger operating cost comparable to buses and trains, making helicopters economical for everyday commuting.

In 1961, the Los Angeles Metropolitan Transit Agency (LAMTA), which operated city buses and was planning a subway system, expressed an interest in helicopters as an additional mass transit mode. Subway stations could have heliports, theorized LAMTA officials. A few LAMTA officials took a demonstration trip on a LAA helicopter, but that was the extent of the agency's involvement with helicopters. By 1967, LAA vice-president Robert Hubley expressed a more realistic viewpoint: "Mass rapid transit is not in the cards in the very near future, but maybe by 1985 or 1990 we may take another look at it."

The city of Pomona built a heliport near its downtown transportation center in early 1968. At the groundbreaking, Belinn said, "The big job is to carry the passenger from his point of origin to his destination without any gaps. This can be done only by a transportation center that intermixes whatever mode is chosen by the customer." Pomona's transportation center provided access to passenger trains, city and regional transit buses, long-distance bus services…and helicopters.

The End of Subsidies

Hoping that helicopter airlines would expand to more cities, the federal government had subsidized the three helicopter airlines since 1954. The subsidies were to be temporary; eventually, the airlines were to become self-sufficient. But several politicians, including President Lyndon B. Johnson, began questioning these subsidies. None of the helicopter airlines, having already received nearly $43 million in subsidies by 1963, was near financial independence. Neither did it seem equitable to subsidize a service used primarily by affluent businessmen while urban mass transit systems, which received little if any government funding, struggled to keep buses and trains running.

Subsidy opponents gained ground when SF-O Helicopter airlines opened in 1961. Founded by several former LAA executives, SF-O linked the cities and airports in the San Francisco Bay Area without a subsidy, primarily

Los Angeles Airways Sikorsky S-61L over Los Angeles. *Courtesy National Air and Space Museum, Smithsonian Institution.*

because its fares were about twice those of LAA. SF-O's founders believed that the helicopter airline was a premium service and should be priced accordingly.

Belinn, along with other helicopter supporters, testified about the importance of keeping the helicopter subsidies. Helicopters provided an essential alternative to travel over crowded streets and highways. And they could be deployed right away, while new highways and mass transit systems would take years, if not decades, to build.

Helicopters had proved their worth during the Korean War and were performing well in Vietnam. The supporters of subsidies argued that the helicopter airlines guaranteed a supply of trained helicopter pilots and mechanics for the military.

Before the Aviation Subcommittee of the U.S. Senate Commerce Committee, Belinn testified, "The economic justification [for helicopter subsidies] is a matter of record. Broad support is needed, however, as the national helicopter operation has become a matter of national concern. Disruption of this service would mark the first time in our country's history when a project such as this has been abandoned for strictly political considerations."

However, Congress voted to end the subsidies by 1965. The Chicago operation ended passenger service. LAA and New York Airways eliminated all but their most productive routes and sought support from the major airlines. LAA also discontinued its mail-only shuttle between downtown Los Angeles and LAX.

THE PARAMOUNT CRASH

From the beginning of passenger service in 1954 until the end of 1967, LAA had carried more than 1.6 million passengers without a major incident.

One day in May 1968, aircraft engineer Lu Zuckerman flew on an LAA helicopter between Disneyland and LAX. He noted the rougher than usual ride quality and, upon landing, noticed that one of the rotor blades was misaligned with the other four. He shared his observation with the ground crew, who assured him that the blade would be repaired during the helicopter's next scheduled maintenance.

A few days later, that same S61-L left Anaheim for LAX at 5:40 p.m. Within ten minutes of takeoff, observers on the ground heard a loud snapping sound. Looking upward, they were horrified to see the helicopter rolling over and over as the tail rotor, and then a main rotor blade, flew off. The helicopter disintegrated as it descended, dropping parts and mail along the way. It crashed into a dairy farm in Paramount, striking the ground tail first and then exploding.

Several bystanders ran to the burning helicopter. They managed to pull one man out, but he had already been decapitated. The intense flames prevented any further rescue attempts. The crash killed all twenty passengers and three crew members on board, making it the deadliest helicopter crash in U.S. history. Among the victims were a family of vacationers; Mayor John Traynor of Red Bluff, California; and Dr. Arden Ruddell, a professor at University of California–Berkeley.

Mail sacks and wreckage were strewn over a 2,500-foot radius. The tail rotor ended up about a block away from the crash site, while the rotor blade pierced the roof of a nearby factory. (No one on the ground was injured.) Firemen and other rescue workers retrieved the bodies and took them to the morgue, while the helicopter parts were moved to a spare hangar at LAX for further investigation.

Los Angeles Airways schedule. *Author's collection.*

LAA grounded all of its flights for a day, while the Federal Aviation Administration made a cursory safety check of the remaining S61-Ls. The Los Angeles County Board of Supervisors, led by Kenneth Hahn, passed a motion asking that all S61-Ls be grounded until the cause of the crash could be found. Rumors that a midair collision or a bomb had destroyed the helicopter proved false.

The National Transportation Safety Board (NTSB) began the painstaking process of determining the exact cause of the crash. Rotor blades had penetrated the fuselage, striking passengers, and had separated the tail rotor from the aircraft. Investigators deciphered a garbled tape of the last communication between the pilot and air traffic control. The pilot was saying, "We're crashing, help us!"

THE COMPTON CRASH

On August 14, Christopher Belinn, the fourteen-year-old grandson of LAA president Clarence Belinn, was traveling via LAA helicopter from his grandparents' house in the San Fernando Valley to his parents' home in Santa Ana. The flight from the Valley to LAX was uneventful. Christopher probably thought of starting school in a few weeks and competing on the track and cross-country teams. He and twenty other passengers boarded the S61-L for the trip to Anaheim. The aircraft lifted off at 10:25 a.m.

About eleven minutes later, witnesses on the ground reported seeing the tail rotor fly off the fuselage and then the helicopter plunging to the ground. It burst into flames as it landed next to Lueders Park in Compton. Observers noticed that the pilot seemed to be doing his best to control the doomed craft so as to land in the park, avoiding nearby houses. Once again, a few brave souls tried to rescue the passengers and crew, but the flames were too hot.

The curious thronged the area as the deputy coroners worked to remove the bodies. Standing by the tail section and doing his best to provide whatever help needed was Clarence Belinn. As he left the area, he said, "My grandson was aboard."

The Compton crash marked the second deadliest in U.S. history, after the Paramount crash. NTSB, which was still investigating the earlier accident, had to handle this mishap as well.

WHAT WENT WRONG

NTSB released its findings for both crashes in 1969. The Paramount crash was caused by the failure of a blade damper, a device attached to each rotor blade to control excessive vibration. Since not all of the parts were recovered

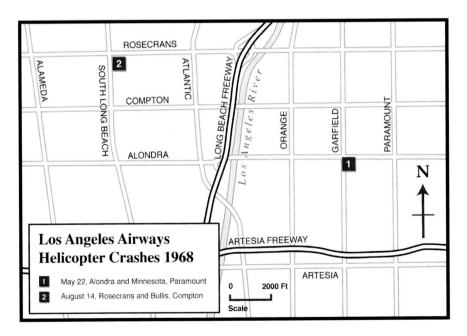

Los Angeles Airways crash site map. *Author's collection/Mapcraft.*

from the crash scene, it was impossible to discover what had caused the blade damper to fail in the first place.

As for the Compton crash, NTSB determined that the spindle linking the rotor blades to the hub had failed due to a crack in the metal, causing one of the blades to break off. With a blade missing, the helicopter became unbalanced, flipped out of control and crashed.

The S61-L's spindles, as part of regularly scheduled maintenance, were to be replaced after every 7,500 flight hours. If a re-manufactured spindle was used, it was to be shot-peened. Vibrations from the helicopter's engine caused microscopic fractures in the metal of the spindle. These fractures would grow into larger, dangerous cracks unless the spindles underwent a process known as shot-peening. In shot-peening, a series of tiny metal, glass or ceramic pellets, about the same diameter as a human hair, are shot at high speed at the metal to be treated. This treatment causes a slight deformation in the target metal, and any fractures are pushed together. Shot-peening also hardens the surface, making it less likely to crack due to metal fatigue.

According to NTSB, the spindle had not been shot-peened adequately, allowing the fractures to become larger and larger until the spindle broke apart.

THE SLOW DECLINE

A week after the Compton crash, LAA resumed regular flights. "We must move ahead. Public demand for our service is great, and we have no choice but to react immediately," said a stoic Belinn.

But crash-fearing passengers stayed away from the helicopters. Ridership dropped from 1967's high of 308,000 passengers to 39,000 in 1968 and fell sharply the following year. The Pomona heliport ticket agent reported that sales plummeted to 5 passengers per day.

Air taxi services, which operated on demand rather than a set schedule, attracted those former LAA passengers still willing to fly in helicopters. Commuter airlines, using small, fixed-wing airplanes capable of taking off from and landing on short runways, were another source of competition. These "short take off and landing" (STOL) aircraft were cheaper to operate than helicopters. LAA leased two DeHavilland Twin-Jet Otters for the San Bernardino route. Belinn considered these airplanes for future expansion to San Diego, Santa Barbara and Palm Springs.

In October 1969, LAA pilots, seeking higher wages and reduced flying hours, went on strike for almost seven months. LAA's post-crash insurance rates quadrupled, while the major airlines, facing financial troubles of their own, withdrew their financial support.

WESTGATE AND HOWARD HUGHES

About one month before the Paramount crash, San Diego–based Westgate-California Corporation attempted to obtain a controlling interest in LAA. But since Westgate already owned Yellow Cab and an airport shuttle bus company, the CAB, citing conflict of interest regulations, barred the company from purchasing part of LAA.

Belinn sought support from industrialist Howard Hughes, who had provided some financial backing to LAA in the past. Hughes offered to buy LAA in 1968 but reneged on the deal two years later. (The initial decision to buy LAA had been made, not by Hughes, but by his head executive Robert Maheu. Other Hughes executives, jealous of Maheu's position, convinced Hughes to cancel the LAA purchase.)

LAA sued Hughes, but it was too late to stop the helicopter airline's financial free fall. LAA suspended all service in January 1971. Golden West Airlines, another commuter carrier, acquired LAA and operated helicopter service on the LAX–Disneyland route for about a year before it, too, went out of business.

Belinn spent the rest of the 1970s in court against Howard Hughes and his companies but lost on appeal in 1979. On December 23, 1988, Belinn passed away.

HELICOPTERS AFTER LAA

After the demise of LAA, several other operators attempted to provide helicopter shuttle service to LAX. On June 4, 1975, Los Angeles Helicopter Airlines started a route between downtown Los Angeles and LAX, using a helipad on top of the Hilton Hotel. Two months later, LAHA added routes to Montebello and Burbank. LAHA also suffered a fatal crash on November 22, 1977, near Burbank. LAHA ended its service in 1979 due to high operating costs and noise complaints.

The most successful post-LAA helicopter airline was Airspur, started by New York Airways founder John Gallagher in September 1983. It flew British-made Westland WG-30 helicopters on routes connecting LAX with Santa Ana (John Wayne Airport), Fullerton and Burbank. Airspur offered joint ticketing with several major airlines.

On November 7, 1983, in a near-repeat of the 1968 LAA Paramount crash, the tail rotor fell off an Airspur helicopter headed from LAX to Orange County. The craft spun out of control, tore through high-voltage power lines and landed a few hundred feet from the I-605 Freeway in Long Beach.

Although no one was killed or seriously injured, Airspur's entire fleet was grounded for two months during NTSB's investigation. The cause of the accident was determined to be a poorly designed lever controlling the tail rotor. After Airspur installed a redesigned rotor, the helicopters returned to the skies in early 1984.

But Airspur continued to have financial problems, and in November, Gallagher sold the airline to Oregon-based Evergreen Aviation. Evergreen was no more successful than Gallagher had been; on February 25, 1985, Airspur turned its last rotor.

Other short-lived helicopter airlines in Southern California included LA Helicopter, founded in 1986 by a former United Airlines pilot, and Helitrans Air Shuttle, which operated between Santa Ana and LAX in the early 1990s. None of these operations came close to providing the frequent commuter service envisioned by Belinn.

New York–based U.S. Helicopter, which had provided scheduled service from Manhattan to JFK and Newark Airports since March 2006, planned to expand to other cities, including Los Angeles. But high costs and the 2008 recession put U.S. Helicopter out of business in early 2009.

Epilogue

No scheduled helicopter service currently operates in Southern California. Island Express flies between Catalina Island and the mainland on a request basis only.

Helicopter noise continues to be an issue. Southern California is much more densely populated than in 1954, when Los Angeles Airways made its first flight. Residents under flight paths have protested against helicopter flights and blocked construction or use of heliports. Also lessening the need for helicopters to LAX is the major airlines' use of suburban airports in Ontario, Santa Ana, Burbank and Long Beach.

The idea of scheduled commuter helicopters must still cross the mind of those stuck in Los Angeles traffic. However, unless technological advances reduce operating costs and noise levels, helicopters will probably never replace conventional ground-based public transportation.

CHAPTER 10

"WATTS WILL HAVE ITS BUS PARTY!"

Dr. Thomas W. Matthew's Blue and White Bus

African Americans have contributed immensely to the transportation history of the United States. Garret Morgan invented the traffic light. Granville T. Woods invented several signaling and operational devices for railroads and streetcars. And Rosa Parks's courageous refusal to give up her bus seat in 1955 led to the modern civil rights movement.

However, one African American transportation pioneer, who had a great deal of influence in the 1960s and early 1970s, is virtually unknown today. Recent African American history books do not mention him; other publications discuss his involvement with Ellis Island or Medicare but not his transportation projects.

DR. THOMAS W. MATTHEW

Thomas William Matthew, born in 1925, was the fifth child and first son of Daniel and Ethel Matthew, both immigrants from the British West Indies. Daniel worked as a janitor in various apartment buildings in the (then) all-white Bronx; he would house his family in the basements of these buildings. Because the nearby hospital did not admit African American patients, Thomas was born in the basement of one of these apartment complexes.

When Tom attended school, he was almost always the only African American student in the class. He often felt the sting of racism. One day in third grade, the teacher read *Little Black Sambo* to the class. "Once upon a time there was a little black boy, and his name was Little Black Sambo. Just like Tommy," she said, pointing at him.

But Tom fought back. As a teenager, he joined the Bronx youth division of the NAACP. Protesting the segregation of New York City parks, he staged a successful sit-in at the parks department, demanding that a vacant lot in the Bronx be converted into a playground for black children.

His strong academic performance enabled him to attend the Bronx High School of Science and then Manhattan College, becoming the first African American to graduate from either school. He continued his education at Meharry Medical College. After graduating in 1949, he performed his internship at St. Louis City Hospital then his residency in Cleveland City Hospital. He hoped to become a neurosurgeon, but he found it nearly impossible to find a program admitting students like him. Finally, the elite Harvard Medical School accepted him in 1951.

In 1955, Dr. Matthew became the first black neurosurgeon trained in the United States. He returned to New York, held positions at Mount Sinai Hospital and became director of neurosurgery at Coney Island Hospital. Dr. Matthew started his own private practice in 1962 and served as a consultant for the New York State Boxing Commission. Despite an office on Park Avenue and a $100,000 yearly income, Dr. Matthew lived modestly in a brownstone in Harlem, enrolled his children in public schools and even refused to buy a third suit for fear of "being ostentatious."

Dr. Matthew continued to be concerned about the poverty, substandard housing and limited access to healthcare affecting black citizens in sections of New York City. In 1963, he used his own money to found Interfaith Hospital, a 140-bed, nonprofit general hospital in Queens. Interfaith was the first hospital in New York State to be owned and operated by African Americans.

SELF-HELP, GROWTH AND RECONSTRUCTION

According to Dr. Matthew, slavery, discrimination and welfare had given many black people a bad attitude toward work. Therefore, he decided to make Interfaith Hospital not only a healthcare facility but also the centerpiece of several work training programs designed to teach people how to be successful in the workforce. These programs would help black citizens and other disadvantaged groups help themselves rather than live on welfare.

In 1964, Dr. Matthew, along with several community leaders, founded the Interfaith Health Association. Later, the association was renamed the National Economic Growth and Reconstruction Organization (N.E.G.R.O.). This organization operated not only Interfaith Hospital but also several other businesses, such as the Domco paint, chemical and textile manufacturing companies and the Spartacus Construction Company. N.E.G.R.O. companies made products used within the organization. Domco Textiles made linens and uniforms for Interfaith Hospital, and the paint factory's products were used to maintain the hospital. Spartacus Construction rehabilitated apartment buildings for N.E.G.R.O.'s housing program and commercial properties for its multiple businesses.

Refurbishments often were done without permits or other official permission. Dr. Matthew felt that laws and regulations such as permit requirements were only "laws of convenience," existing only to protect special-interest groups. Such laws, Dr. Matthew contended, were "not vital to society's survival" and "inherently discriminatory," as they kept black residents and other disadvantaged minorities from providing for their needs.

In the tradition of civil disobedience, Dr. Matthew was willing to break those laws, and pay any penalties incurred, if he believed it was in the interest of the African American community. Relations between Dr. Matthew and the city and state governments were contentious. Sometimes he would have his employees barricade buildings, preventing city inspectors or other officials from gaining access, as a form of protest.

To finance his projects, while avoiding the appearance of direct governmental help, N.E.G.R.O. sold "Economic Liberty Bonds," or "N.E.G.R.O. Bonds." These bonds were sold in denominations ranging from $0.25 to $10,000.00 and would mature in ten years. Dr. Matthew encouraged all sectors of society to buy the bonds. "You don't have to be black to buy N.E.G.R.O. bonds," he would often say.

However, Dr. Matthew did accept federal Medicare funds for providing patient care at the hospital, as well as Small Business Administration (SBA) funds for the work-training businesses. He even obtained contracts with the U.S. military to produce clothing and chemicals.

DR. MATTHEW STARTS A BUS LINE

Many of Dr. Matthew's patients and workers did not own automobiles and relied on public transportation. However, the bus and subway lines in Queens, Harlem and other disadvantaged neighborhoods required several transfers. To improve transportation access to Interfaith Hospital and his other programs, Dr. Matthew started his own bus line. He acquired a few used buses and hired drivers, and on July 25, 1967, the first Blue and White buses went into service in Queens, linking Linden Avenue with Interfaith Hospital.

Blue and White Bus operated without a franchise from New York City. Dr. Matthew and city officials fought constantly over his right to operate the buses. He considered the franchise requirement another discriminatory "law of convenience" and vowed to continue the bus service. "Detroit is burning with $300-million worth of damage in a 'hot' riot," he said. "What we are in the process of doing is creating a 'cool' riot. The cool riot, which we purposefully undertake, is doing things that will be productive for our group and all society, but couldn't be done through bureaucratic red tape."

A Blue and White bus in New York. *Courtesy Johnson Publishing Company, LLC. All rights reserved.*

In early 1968, the New York State Supreme Court ordered Dr. Matthew to stop running his buses. Dr. Matthew stated, "Judge or no judge, court order or no court order, the bus will continue to run," and started an additional route in Harlem.

Watts or Bus(t)

By 1966, Dr. Matthew had given up his private practice in favor of focusing his full attention on his fast-growing, self-help organization. He considered expanding N.E.G.R.O. to other parts of the United States before looking at the Watts neighborhood of Los Angeles.

In August 1965, a confrontation between Marquette Frye, a twenty-two-year-old African American, and a California Highway Patrol officer led to six days of rioting in Watts, leaving thirty-four dead, more than three thousand arrested and two hundred buildings destroyed. Both the leaders and citizens of Los Angeles, who associated race riots with older cities such as New York, Chicago and Detroit, wondered how one could happen in placid Southern California.

A state commission's report, produced by former CIA director John McCone, told another story. The black population of Watts, which had grown during and after World War II, faced discrimination and police harassment on a daily basis. Prevented by racially restrictive real estate covenants from moving elsewhere, they had to put up with substandard housing and lack of access to jobs, education and healthcare. Underlying these issues was the lack of adequate public transportation.

Public Transportation in Watts

Public transit ridership in and around Watts was high, since relatively few people owned automobiles. When the last Pacific Electric Red Car was replaced by bus service in April 1961, commuters' trip times from Watts to Los Angeles were nearly doubled. Express buses provided high-speed service between Los Angeles and Long Beach via the new Harbor and Long Beach Freeways, but these routes bypassed Watts.

Since the mid-1920s, two local bus companies had served the area. Frank Atkinson and his son, Herbert, owned the South Los Angeles Transportation Company, which provided north–south service from a terminal at Broadway and Manchester, along Main, Central or Avalon, to downtown Compton. At Broadway and Manchester, passengers could transfer to Los Angeles Railway's #7 streetcar (replaced by a bus in 1955) for service into downtown Los Angeles. The Atkinsons participated in the civic life of Watts and hired African American employees. During the 1965 riot, only one of their buses had been damaged.

The Atkinson Transit Company, also owned by Frank and Herbert Atkinson, had four routes radiating from 103rd Street and Compton Boulevard, at the heart of the Watts shopping district. Three of the routes extended from Watts to nearby Huntington Park, the Florence district and Compton. The Atkinsons acquired the routes in 1953 from Felicien P. Landier (Landier Transit). While South Los Angeles Transportation and Atkinson Transit were operated as separate entities due to differing labor contracts, passengers enjoyed free transfers between the two systems.

The Los Angeles Metropolitan Transit Authority (LAMTA), which became the Southern California Rapid Transit District (RTD) in 1964, provided limited service. CPUC prohibited LAMTA or RTD from establishing routes in direct competition with any existing public transportation provider. The Atkinsons' bus routes, therefore, prevented most RTD service from penetrating south of Manchester Boulevard. These restrictions were confusing and annoying to bus passengers.

Frank Atkinson, in his mid-seventies and eager to retire, expressed interest in selling the bus companies. However, his son, Herbert, genuinely concerned about the difficulties his passengers faced in traveling to downtown Los Angeles, was more interested in expanding service. Herbert sought to extend the Avalon Boulevard route, via a nonstop express route, into central Los Angeles and San Pedro, but he was blocked by the existing transit companies, which did not want competition on their routes to downtown.

Blue and White Bus of Watts

Dr. Matthew, vowing to improve bus service in Watts with or without a franchise, offered nearly $500,000 for the Atkinson bus systems. This offer

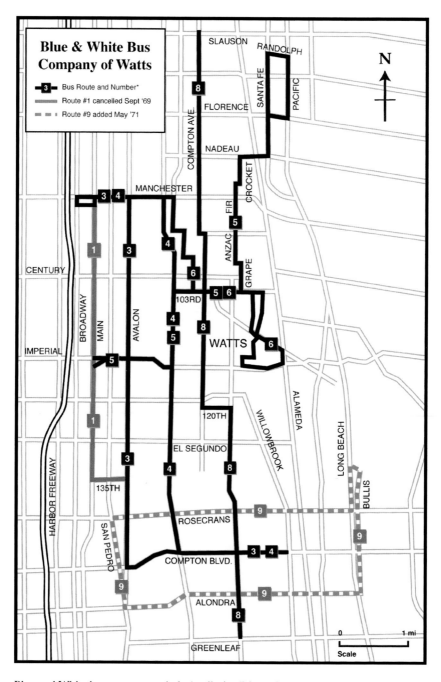

Blue and White bus route map. *Author's collection/Mapcraft.*

proved acceptable to Frank and Herb, and in December 1967, Dr. Matthew acquired both the South Los Angeles Transit Company and the Atkinson Transit System. He merged the two companies under the name Blue and White Bus Company of Watts and retained Herb as manager.

Dr. Matthew, having ended bus service in New York, had twelve buses driven overland to Watts. On the way, one of the buses collided with an automobile. Dr. Matthew, on board another bus, performed a life-saving operation using a ballpoint pen to hold the auto driver's airway open.

Most of these buses broke down along the way; only three made it to Watts. Dr. Matthew declared that an additional twenty-seven buses were arriving by rail and promised not only improved service but also a board of community members to advise the bus company.

To strengthen the bus company's financial condition, Dr. Matthew raised fares by a nickel. In July 1969, he asked CPUC for permission to cancel Route #1 (Main Street). Ridership along this route was low because the riot had destroyed many of the businesses on Main Street.

DR. MATTHEW AND PRESIDENT NIXON

Dr. Matthew's pro-capitalist philosophies attracted the attention of political speechwriter Patrick Buchanan, who in 1966 introduced him to former vice president Richard Milhous Nixon. When Nixon became president, he wanted and needed the support of the African American community, though he did not wish to offend his base of conservative voters by promoting welfare-based programs. In Dr. Matthew and N.E.G.R.O., Nixon found a cause to champion, while the doctor became one of his biggest supporters.

In March 1968, the federal government charged Dr. Matthew with tax evasion. He freely admitted not paying $103,000 in income taxes and stated that he used the money to fund his self-help projects rather than giving it to the government for more welfare programs. He was convicted on October 20, 1969, and sentenced to five years at a federal prison in Danbury, Connecticut. However, Dr. Matthew had served a mere three months before Nixon, in his first act of clemency, pardoned him on January 6, 1970.

Nixon ordered members of his administration to "provide all possible support to Dr. Matthew." Later, it would be discovered that administration officials had put pressure on other government agencies to ignore any problems with Interfaith Hospital and to suppress or destroy evidence showing that Dr. Matthew had misused government funds.

THE WATTS BUS PARTY

RTD, in response to the McCone Commission's recommendations, expanded its bus route system in Watts and South Central Los Angeles. New routes provided east–west service along Century Boulevard and Imperial Highway and connected Watts with affluent West Los Angeles, Beverly Hills and Pacific Palisades.

Because east–west bus routes south of Manchester Boulevard were few, RTD added a new east–west route, #123 along El Segundo Boulevard, on February 8, 1971. This route provided access to the El Segundo aerospace firms in El Segundo and to St. Francis Hospital in Lynwood. The route crossed four of Blue and White's north–south routes.

Dr. Matthew considered Route #123 an illegal violation of Blue and White's service area and declared that the transit agency was trying to "destroy the people's self-help bus line." He provided a six-point list of demands to RTD:

> *RTD would voluntarily cancel Route #123, or any other route in Blue and White's service area*
> *RTD would lend Blue and White $3 million in operating capital*
> *RTD would lend-lease 20 new buses to Blue and White*
> *RTD would enter into a million-dollar contract for Watts to wash all of its buses for the next five years*
> *RTD would turn over all its bus routes in Watts to the black community*
> *RTD would enter into a "cultural exchange agreement" with Blue and White*

Although some RTD officials expressed sympathy with these requests, the agency lacked legal authority to give money, equipment or bus routes to a private entity such as Blue and White. Dr. Matthew was not satisfied with RTD's response to his demands. "Boston had its tea party, Watts will have its bus party!" he thundered.

On February 9, 1971, drivers on RTD's Route #3, which served Sixth Street, downtown Los Angeles and Central Avenue, noticed that they were

Thomas W. Matthew at Blue and White Bus yard in Watts. *UCLA Charles E. Young Department of Special Collections,* Los Angeles Times *Photographic Archives.*

sharing the route with a bus of a different color. Two Blue and White buses were seen operating along the route, cutting in front of RTD buses and boarding passengers for free. While on board, Blue and White officials lectured the passengers on the feud between the two companies and asked them to support Blue and White.

Although one of the Blue and White buses nearly struck a police officer, neither the police nor RTD made any effort to stop them, possibly fearing that a confrontation with Dr. Matthew would be publicized by the media.

Blue and White buses similarly shadowed Route #123 buses on El Segundo Boulevard. One RTD driver reported being harassed by Blue and White employees or supporters. In a February 12 letter to RTD, Dr. Matthew wrote, "The operation of free Blue and White service on your #3 route will continue and will extend as we see fit to other RTD lines. Should you decide to cease your illegal action and wish to negotiate the disagreement between RTD and Blue and White, we will, of course, be happy to meet with you."

Blue and White operated its service over RTD Route #3 throughout February, while RTD continued to defend its Route #123 as legal because it provided a needed service under the recommendations of the McCone report. Only a few passengers on Route #123 would have chosen to use Blue and White buses instead, according to RTD.

DR. MATTHEW: HERE, THERE AND EVERYWHERE

As the N.E.G.R.O. businesses reached their peak in 1970, Dr. Matthew involved himself in several other projects. The most ambitious was improvements to Ellis Island, the historic entry point for millions of immigrants, including Dr. Matthew's parents. However, since the mid-1950s, the buildings on the island had fallen into disrepair. Dr. Matthew planned to restore the buildings and then provide drug rehabilitation and job training programs, as well as tourist activities, on the island. After a thirteen-day demonstration in July 1970, when Dr. Matthew and sixty-three others occupied the island, the National Park Service gave N.E.G.R.O. a five-year contract to repair the buildings. But restoring the dilapidated facilities became a bigger job than Dr. Matthew anticipated; by September 1971, N.E.G.R.O. had abandoned the project.

In July 1971, Dr. Matthew led a delegation of nineteen N.E.G.R.O. employees to the Soviet Union to investigate the treatment of Russian Jews, comparing their situation with that of black citizens in the United States. Soviet officials, however, were not supportive of his efforts, and he returned after two days, rather than the six weeks he had planned.

Dr. Matthew was seemingly in several places at once, flying to Los Angeles to deal with Blue and White and then back to New York to manage the hospital and the Domco businesses. He started micromanaging the businesses and overextending himself. Business practices and financial accounting were careless; funds earmarked for one program were often shifted, either deliberately or inadvertently, to another.

Dr. Matthew's connection with Nixon, as well as his own political beliefs, led him to support George Harold Carswell for Supreme Court justice, even though Carswell had supported segregation. Dr. Matthew, insisting that Carswell had been "rehabilitated" from his views in the same manner an addict could be rehabilitated from drugs, bought full-page newspaper ads supporting Carswell's confirmation. He also disagreed publicly with other African American political groups such as the NAACP, even staging noisy demonstrations at the NAACP office. These actions alienated Dr. Matthew from mainstream black leadership. By this time, most African Americans were on the side of the NAACP and similar organizations and had little use for Dr. Matthew's politics or programs.

BLUE AND WHITE WEEK IN COMPTON

The city of Compton, about three miles south of Watts, underwent a demographic change after the 1965 riots. Whites moved away, and African Americans started moving in.

Compton was served by three Blue and White routes and a few meandering RTD lines. Dr. Matthew, without asking permission from CPUC, added new Blue and White Route #9 in Compton on May 24, 1971.

The city staged a ceremony to inaugurate the new bus route. The Compton High School band played, a youth dance company performed and Mayor Douglas Dollarhide declared the week "Blue and White Bus Week." He stated that Route #9 would "increase the community's financial capability" by allowing greater access to jobs. Again, CPUC warned Dr. Matthew that the route lacked proper authorization but did nothing to stop it.

END OF THE LINE

Blue and White's financial condition only worsened. In late June, the company failed to pay insurance premiums and lost coverage. Once CPUC found out, it suspended Blue and White's operating certificate, making operations illegal until insurance was restored. But the buses rolled on.

Blue and White's drivers, represented by the United Transportation Union, went on strike July 17 after the banks returned their paychecks for insufficient funds. "The buses will run even if we have to run over them," threatened a Blue and White official. Strikebreakers, some of whom may have been "recovering addicts" from Interfaith Hospital, were hired to drive buses. Union drivers and strikebreakers argued, and some buses were vandalized. Blue and White operated about half of its regular scheduled service. Some of the buses were more than twenty years old, and breakdowns were common. On August 10, county marshals impounded the buses, keeping them off the street for two days until the union drivers had been fully paid.

On September 10, Internal Revenue Service agents stopped the buses, ordered all passengers to deboard and then towed the vehicles to an impound lot in Bell. Blue and White had failed to pay federal income taxes.

By this time, the community only wanted reliable bus service. And RTD was ready to provide it. The day after Blue and White's buses were impounded, RTD hired the original Blue and White drivers and mechanics and began replacement service on all the former Blue and White routes, except for the unauthorized Route #9.

Dr. Matthew vowed to reinstate Blue and White, with new routes serving downtown Los Angeles and Disneyland. After a disastrous attempt at charter bus service, the company went out of business in 1972.

WHAT ABOUT INTERFAITH?

Conditions at Interfaith Hospital, once the centerpiece of Dr. Matthew's organization, deteriorated until it became little more than an abandoned building housing a handful of "recovering" addicts but devoid of any medical staff. The hospital had also become a public nuisance. Several fistfights and a homicide at the hospital triggered an investigation that led to its closure and exposed financial irregularities in all of Dr. Matthew's businesses.

On November 7, 1973, Dr. Matthew was convicted of diverting federal Medicaid funds intended for Interfaith to other projects, including Blue and White. Claiming that the funds went to "industrial clinics" for treating recovering drug addicts, he appealed his conviction, and on March 3, 1975, it was overturned. But his organization was now in shambles. The Domco textile and chemical factories were closed and their equipment repossessed to repay the SBA loans, which were now in default. And President Nixon's resignation in August 1974 over the Watergate scandal left Dr. Matthew without any political allies. He returned to medical practice and disappeared from public view.

EPILOGUE

Although many disadvantaged people may have been helped by his programs, irregular bus service, understaffed health facilities and other half-completed projects undoubtedly hurt others. Dr. Matthew's organization was just too ambitious to be sustainable. "Yes, I think I overextended myself," he admitted in a 1973 *New York Times* interview. After the Blue and White Bus takeover, RTD (now Metro) expanded service, implemented a grid network of bus routes and opened the Metro Blue and Green light rail lines. Local bus systems—such as Watts DASH, Willowbrook Link and Compton Renaissance Transit—serve residential streets and other areas unserved by Metro.

CHAPTER 11

GROOVY BUSES TO THE BEACH

The Kadletz Brothers and the Pink Bus Line

On a warm summer morning in 1971, a small group of teenagers waits on Beach Boulevard, arms outstretched and thumbs pointed up, for a ride to Huntington Beach. They are all too young to drive, and all of their parents work or are otherwise too busy to drive them to the beach, so hitchhiking is the only way to get around—or is it?

In the distance, one of the teens notices a pink-and-white bus getting closer. Within a few minutes, it rolls up to the curb and stops. It is full of chattering teenagers with their surfboards and beach gear. The bus door opens, and the driver, who looks almost as young as his passengers, calls out, "Going to the beach?"

The group walks toward the bus. "Hey, wait a minute," yells one teen. "Buses cost money." He turns to the driver. "How much?"

"From here, a dollar twenty." The teens dig into pockets and purses, find the required fare and board the bus, sending the coins clanking into the farebox before finding a seat. The ride is nothing but fun, with other teens to chat with and rock music booming from the onboard stereo.

Finally, the bus arrives at its last stop: the beach. "Last bus back is at 6:00 p.m.," the driver warns as the bus empties.

THE KADLETZ BROTHERS AND THE PINK BUS

Michael Kadletz and his younger brother, Paul, spent their childhoods in the northern Orange County city of Brea during the 1960s. As teenagers, they often joined the group of young people hitchhiking to the beach on warm summer days.

After seeing the throngs of teenagers with their thumbs out, year after year, the two brothers decided that a bus to the beach not only would be safer but also would be profitable. Orange County bus service consisted of regional Southern California Rapid Transit District routes, carrying passengers to Los Angeles, Long Beach, Santa Ana and San Bernardino. North–south service along the county's street grid was nonexistent. The new Orange County Transit District, voted into existence in 1970, did not operate any buses yet.

The Kadletzes proposed a simple twenty-one-mile line on Beach Boulevard, running from Whittier Boulevard in La Habra and then southward through the cities of Buena Park, Anaheim, Stanton, Garden Grove and Westminster before ending at Pacific Coast Highway in Huntington Beach.

Mike and Paul Kadletz promote the Pink Bus. *UCLA Charles E. Young Department of Special Collections*, Los Angeles Times *Photographic Archives.*

In 1970, using funds earned at a part-time supermarket job, Mike and Paul purchased two used 1954-model buses from American International Bus Exchange for $750 each. But they thought that the green-and-yellow paint scheme of the former Gardena Municipal Bus Lines vehicles was ugly, so they painted the buses an attention-getting pink and white, using house paint and a rented compressor.

To promote the new service, the Kadletzes bartered ads on and in the buses for ad space in newspapers and commercial time on radio stations. They also printed bumper stickers. Motorola provided free sound systems for the buses as a promotion for its stereos.

Convincing CPUC

Upon discussions with the cities, however, the Kadletzes learned that in order to legally operate the bus service, they would need a certificate from the California Public Utilities Commission (CPUC).

Initially, CPUC officials were not convinced that the two brothers had the experience to run a bus line. "They laughed in our faces," said Mike. But, undeterred, Mike and Paul set about to obtain the necessary certificate. They filled out a twenty-seven-page application, submitted it and waited. Officials from CPUC met with the Kadletzes in April to determine whether their proposed bus company would be financially stable enough to keep operating for at least three years.

"You can't go into the bus business on a fly-by-night approach," chided a CPUC staffer. The brothers planned to charge up to $0.60 for a ride along the entire line from La Habra to Huntington Beach; CPUC staffers convinced them that the fare needed to be doubled to $1.20.

Finally, CPUC granted a certificate to Pink Bus Lines on June 2, 1971. However, the Kadletzes still had trouble acquiring the required insurance coverage. The insurance company insisted that bus drivers be at least twenty-five years old. (At nineteen and seventeen, Mike and Paul were too young to drive their own buses!) The insurer's reluctance to issue a policy delayed Pink Bus service for a few days. Only after a call from CPUC did the insurer provide the necessary coverage, allowing the Pink Bus to start rolling.

FIRST DAY OF SERVICE

The first Pink Bus left Whittier and Beach Boulevards on June 25, at 7:00 a.m. More than 225 teenagers rode the bus that day. The first bus filled up quickly, forcing the brothers to put their second bus on the street as fast as possible.

Once prospective passengers learned about the Pink Bus, all they had to do was walk to Beach Boulevard, wait for the bus and wave at it to stop. Once on board, riders enjoyed a party-like atmosphere. The buses' sound systems played the latest hit songs. Alternatively, a rider might strum a guitar and serenade everyone. In the teen slang of the time, the kids thought riding the Pink Bus was "groovy."

"The kids are great," said driver Jerry Meng. "They don't tear up the seats and they just sit back and dig the sounds."

Riders who did not have the fare for the trip back home could leave their surfboard, swim fins or other equipment with the bus driver as collateral and pay the next day.

About 250 to 275 passengers caught the Pink Bus on weekdays, but weekend ridership was much less; apparently, teens obtained rides from their parents on weekends. The Pink Bus also attracted quite a few senior citizens, mostly on the "reverse" trips (northward from Huntington Beach in the morning and southward in the afternoons).

September came, and Pink Bus's young patrons went back to school. The Kadletzes reduced service to operate on Monday, Wednesday and Friday only; by September 17, service was suspended entirely. The brothers had made $14,000, before expenses. "Business would have been better yet if the PUC hadn't delayed us. We didn't have time to advertise before the end of school," remarked Mike.

FREEDOM BUS LINES

The Kadletzes wanted to continue providing bus service during times when the beach runs were unprofitable. In October, they started Freedom Bus Lines, a shuttle bus in Buena Park serving attractions such as Knott's Berry Farm, the Japanese Deer Park and Movieland Wax Museum. Buses painted in a patriotic scheme of red, white and blue

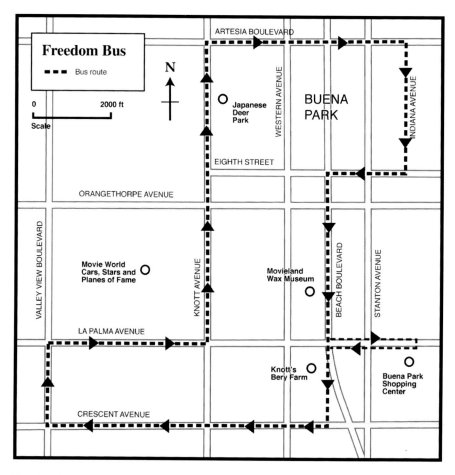

Freedom Bus Lines route map. *Author's collection/Mapcraft.*

looped through town every hour. Freedom Bus Lines operated until May 1972.

The Pink Bus Goes to College

Another source of year-round income came from university campus shuttles. In 1972, OCTD and the University of California–Irvine provided a $6,000 grant to Pink Bus Lines to provide a shuttle service to and from campus.

Parking at UCI was limited, and existing South Coast Transit bus service was very infrequent. Many students chose to hitchhike.

The fare-free UCI shuttle, which started in September, operated in a one-way loop between campus and Newport Beach, stopping at student apartment complexes along the way. Occasionally, a professor would hold an impromptu discussion session onboard, turning the bus into a rolling classroom.

Although the shuttle was intended for faculty, staff and students, drivers picked up anyone along the route who wanted to ride. South Coast Transit, whose routes the Pink Bus partially duplicated, complained that the free Pink Bus service was illegal competition. The university then declared the Pink Bus shuttle a "school bus" and noted that it would only transport students (no faculty, staff or visitors allowed). South Coast Transit, still not mollified, filed a protest with CPUC against UCI and Pink Bus on January 27, 1973. Eventually, UCI was able to convince both the transit company and CPUC that non-students would not be carried, and South Coast Transit dropped its protest in May.

By February, Pink's UCI shuttle was carrying about three hundred passengers per day. While buses ran full in the morning, afternoon runs were less productive. Because the route was a one-way loop, a student living close to campus might have a ten-minute ride to class but would have to endure a thirty- to forty-minute ride back home. Some students would ride one way and then hitchhike for the return trip. Bus breakdowns happened often; the driver was usually forced to attempt a quick repair, as backup buses were rarely available.

The Pink Bus shuttle continued until the end of the school year in June. By the time classes resumed in September 1973, OCTD had acquired South Coast Transit and improved service to UCI, so the Pink Bus shuttle was no longer needed.

In 1973, the Kadletzes acquired the San Diego State University's Bug Line, which connected the campus to San Diego's beaches. Journalism professor Jack Haberstroh, concerned about student hitchhiking, started the fare-free Bug Line in 1972 as a class project. Students drove and repaired the buses, which were decorated as gigantic insects with huge fiberglass eyes and antennae. Students also sold advertising to cover the bus line's costs. However, operating responsibilities became too much for Haberstroh and his students to handle, so he sold the Bug Line to the Kadletzes.

The Kadletzes added to the buses trailers capable of carrying fourteen bicycles. However, drivers' wages (Pink Bus used professional drivers instead of volunteer students) and rising fuel costs required that a ten-dollar monthly fare be charged. The fare, plus improvements in San Diego Transit's local bus service, caused Bug Line ridership to fall. After school ended in June 1974, the Bug Line was canceled.

HARBOR BOULEVARD

OCTD continued to add routes. On April 13, 1973, the agency started a new line on Harbor Boulevard, linking Fullerton to Newport Beach. OCTD also planned a route on Beach Boulevard but was legally barred from operating service competing with a private bus operator. If OCTD wanted to operate on Beach Boulevard, where Pink Bus Lines already operated, it would have to acquire Pink Bus first. By law, the purchase price had to be at least the average revenue over the past three years. But the Kadletzes wanted a much higher price for their bus line.

On the other hand, the Kadletzes were concerned that an OCTD route along Harbor Boulevard, four miles east of the Pink Bus route, would attract their passengers. The Kadletzes filed not only a protest with CPUC against OCTD's Harbor Boulevard proposed line but also an application for their own new route on Harbor.

"They consider that anything within five miles will divert passengers from their line," complained OCTD general manager Pete Fielding. However, Mike Kadletz noted that passengers in northern Orange County could still take advantage of the new OCTD line by riding La Habra's dial-a-ride (a small bus, operating like a taxi) to a Harbor Boulevard bus stop and then transferring to the OCTD bus to Newport Beach. OCTD charged $0.50 for this trip, as opposed to Pink Bus's $1.20 fare for a ride from La Habra to Huntington Beach.

"We'd like to remain in business and could do so, if the Transit District does not begin a north–south run that would compete with us," said Mike Kadletz. But he was also considering selling the Pink Bus to OCTD at an undisclosed price.

OCTD director John Kanel, surmising that the Kadletzes' Harbor Boulevard application was engineered to force OCTD to acquire the company, remarked, "They may be young and operate old buses, but I don't see them as martyrs like some of the newspapers picture them. I'd say they are pretty sharp operators."

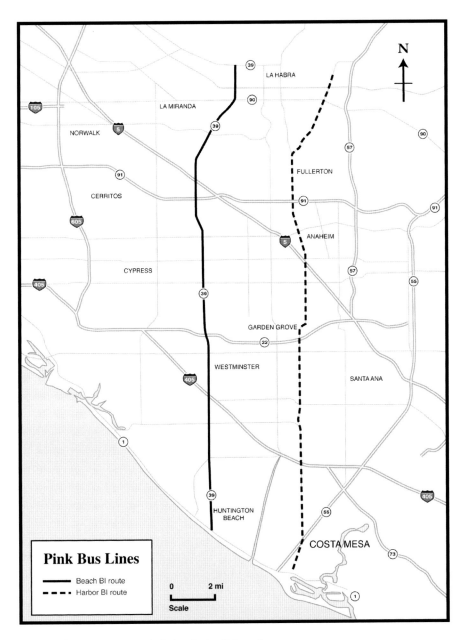

Pink Bus Lines route map. *Author's collection/Mapcraft.*

On May 14, OCTD, which had offered to purchase Pink Bus Lines for $30,000, raised its offer to $32,000. The Kadletzes had until May 22 to either accept or reject the offer.

By June, OCTD officials, losing their patience with the Kadletzes, made a final offer to Pink Bus. If the Kadletzes refused the offer, OCTD would take them to arbitration to determine a price for the bus line. If arbitration failed, the next step would be court action to acquire Pink Bus through condemnation, and a court would set the price OCTD would pay for Pink Bus.

The Kadletzes, however, refused OCTD's final offer, claiming that it would not compensate them for expected fare revenues of about $30,000 for the upcoming summer season. Instead, they sued the transit district, seeking an injunction to stop the transit district from operating its Harbor Boulevard route. They claimed that Pink Bus Lines was losing $1,000 per week due to competition from OCTD and was in danger of shutting down.

On August 6, OCTD and the Kadletzes finally reached an agreement. OCTD would buy Pink Bus Lines' "objection rights" for $24,000. This meant that Pink Bus and OCTD could both operate along Beach and Harbor Boulevards, without Pink Bus objecting to the presence of OCTD service. Also, both OCTD's condemnation suit and Pink Bus Lines' charges of unfair competition would be dropped. Pink Bus service on Harbor Boulevard started on July 26, with four round trips per day. OCTD began its Beach Boulevard service on September 11, after Pink Bus Lines had ceased operations for the season.

OF AARDVARKS AND TEUTERBERGS:
END OF THE PINK BUS LINE

During the struggles with OCTD, Paul Kadletz, deciding to pursue other interests, sold his share of Pink Bus Lines to Howard Ahmanson Jr., son of Home Savings founder Howard Ahmanson. Pink Bus Lines acquired five additional used buses shortly thereafter. Mike Kadletz, along with his new partner, planned to expand next summer's beach bus service northward from La Habra to Hacienda Heights and open a new route to Pomona.

Instead, in April 1974, Mike and Howard sold the Pink Bus Lines to Alwin Teuterberg, who renamed the company Aardvark Bus Lines. Teuterberg was only interested in operating charter bus service. By this time, OCTD was providing regular service on Beach Boulevard, and the Pink Bus became a fading memory.

Good Time Tours: David Fights Goliath Again

In 1977, Mike started Good Time Tours, a sightseeing bus company that picked up passengers at Orange County hotels and took them on tours of Palm Springs.

Much to his dismay, the large, internationally known Gray Line Tours started its own Orange County–Palm Springs tour. Gray Line, whose rights to operate such a tour predated World War II, had not done so since 1965. Gray Line, being much better known than the fledgling Good Time, ended up getting most of the tour business, causing severe financial difficulties for Mike's company.

Mike filed a complaint to CPUC against Gray Line. Not only did he think it was unfair that Gray Line could leave its operating rights dormant for years and then suddenly reactivate them, but he also felt that he had put thousands of dollars into Good Time and Gray Line was taking advantage of his efforts.

CPUC agreed. Its precedent-setting ruling noted, "Unused operating authority should be revoked. It is not equitable nor in the public interest for carriers to retain or collect unused operating authority which they can activate or put in dormant status at will." Gray Line's authority was revoked, but it was too late for Good Time Tours; the financial damage had been done. Good Time ceased operating in early 1980.

Epilogue

Although out of the scheduled and charter bus business, Mike Kadletz's interest in buses has remained strong over the years. Nowadays, instead of operating buses, he converts them into luxury motor homes. Since 1991, he has published *Bus Conversions*, a magazine for people converting old buses to motor homes.

The Orange County Transit District became the Orange County Transportation Authority in 1991. Its Route #29 provides frequent service on Beach Boulevard between La Habra and Huntington Beach. On a warm summer day, a few beachgoers with surfboards, coolers and other beach gear will ride. But OCTA #29 is nowhere near as quirky as the bright pink buses cruising along Beach Boulevard, with their stereos on full blast and drivers almost as young as their passengers.

CHAPTER 12

DIAMONDS ARE FOREVER

Adriana Gianturco and the Diamond Lane

Nearly every freeway in Southern California features a carpool lane. Otherwise known as "High Occupancy Vehicle" (HOV) or "Diamond" lanes, they offer a faster trip for those commuters willing to give up the convenience of driving solo.

While most commuters, carpoolers or not, now accept carpool lanes, the first attempt to provide them on a Southern California freeway in 1976 was met with anger, protests and lawsuits. The Santa Monica Freeway Diamond Lane Project was ended in a matter of months, and it would be nearly a decade before another carpool lane opened. Finally, the project also altered the career course of Adriana Gianturco, the first woman appointed director of a state highway department.

ADRIANA GIANTURCO

Born in Berkeley, California, on June 5, 1939, Adriana Gianturco was the oldest child of Elio and Valentina McGillicuddy Gianturco. A year later, the Gianturcos moved to Washington, D.C. Adriana grew up on the East Coast. She attended Smith College before returning to California in 1960 for a master's degree in economics at the University of California–Berkeley.

After graduation, her attempts to find work met with much discrimination, and there was little open to her but secretarial jobs. Having been asked, "How fast do you type?" too many times, she decided to seek employment outside of the United States. She traveled through the Middle East and Europe, eventually settling in Paris, where she worked as a reporter for *Time* magazine for two years.

In 1964, Gianturco returned to the United States and enrolled in the urban planning program at Harvard University. While in Boston, she worked for two nonprofit social service agencies, Planning Services Group and Action for Boston Community Development, and then became director of planning at the Massachusetts Office of State Planning and Development. In all of these organizations, she worked to preserve older neighborhoods by stopping freeway construction. She also met John Saltonstall Jr., a Boston city councilman. They married in early 1970.

CALIFORNIA HIGHWAYS: END OF AN ERA?

The big boom of freeway construction had taken place in the 1950s and '60s. Engineers drew lines on maps, put contracts out to bid and started up the bulldozers. Gasoline taxes provided plenty of funds for construction. Freeways were built with minimal regard for existing land use. The multi-lane roads cut through mountains, open space, wetlands and neighborhoods, but construction was heavily supported by local government officials as a source of jobs, an impetus for development and a visible result of the taxes paid to Washington and Sacramento. Freeway construction satisfied engineers, politicians, the "highway lobby" (automobile, tire and oil companies), land developers and, at least initially, the general public.

By the early 1970s, however, Californians had begun expressing concerns over the environmental and social effects of freeways. Construction was disruptive and uprooted residents, and when finished, the freeways generated noise and air pollution. They also cut neighborhoods in half.

"Freeway Revolts" took place across the state, making it increasingly difficult to plan or build any more freeways. Additionally, funding from gasoline taxes became less able to cover the ever-increasing costs of construction. That meant less work for the highway engineers. Some of them were laid off, leaving the remaining engineers demoralized.

The California Department of Highways became the California Department of Transportation (Caltrans) in 1973, reflecting the state's interest in planning for other modes of transportation, such as public transit, intercity rail and pedestrian and bicycle facilities. The highway engineers, who had spent most of their careers designing and planning new freeways, grumbled about the shift in the department's priorities.

JERRY BROWN AND APPOINTMENT

On November 5, 1974, Jerry Brown was elected to his first term as California governor. He made an effort to appoint women, minorities and environmentalists to important government positions. Gianturco, who had met Brown while attending UC–Berkeley, was in Boston completing her PhD in urban planning. She had only her dissertation left to complete when Governor Brown appointed her as director of Caltrans.

Adriana Gianturco. *UCLA Charles E. Young Department of Special Collections,* Los Angeles Times *Photographic Archives.*

High Occupancy Vehicle Lanes

Interest in HOV lanes began in the early '60s. Increasing traffic congestion, along with pressure from the U.S. Environmental Protection Agency (EPA) to reduce automobile emissions, led transportation and governmental officials to promote alternatives to driving alone. "Move people, not cars" became the rallying cry.

The first HOV lane in the United States was a twelve-mile, reversible bus–only lane on the Shirley Highway (I-395) between Northern Virginia and Washington, D.C. In Southern California, the El Monte Busway, eleven miles of bus-only lanes on the San Bernardino Freeway (I-10) between El Monte and Los Angeles, opened in January 1973.

In December 1973, the California State Senate passed a resolution (SCR 84) directing the state department of transportation to implement a HOV lane program. By 1974, the State of California, County of Los Angeles and City of Los Angeles had chosen the Santa Monica Freeway for a pilot project. During morning and evening rush hours, the freeway lanes closest to the median (the "fast" lanes) would be reserved for buses and carpools carrying three or more people. These lanes would be marked with diamonds, the symbol used to mark HOV lanes elsewhere in the United States.

In addition to the reserved lanes, ramp meters, or special traffic signals, were installed at each on-ramp in April 1975. These signals limited the number of cars allowed to merge onto the freeway, keeping traffic free flowing.

Because of a labor dispute with the Southern California Rapid Transit District (RTD) bus driver union, the opening date of the Diamond Lane, originally planned for June 15, 1975, was delayed until March 15, 1976—just in time for Gianturco's first day as director of Caltrans.

The Diamond Lane's First Day

For Santa Monica Freeway commuters, that day could only be described as chaos. The Diamond Lanes provided a faster ride for those who could carpool or take the bus. For everyone else, who now had only three lanes to cram into, it was a different story.

Left: Traffic crowds into remaining mixed-flow lanes, while Diamond Lane traffic moves quickly. *UCLA Charles E. Young Department of Special Collections,* Los Angeles Times *Photographic Archives.*

Below: Santa Monica Municipal Bus Lines #10 (Diamond Lane route). *Courtesy Santa Monica Big Blue Bus.*

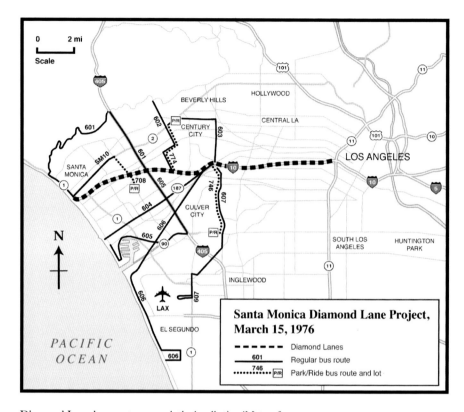

Diamond Lane bus route map. *Author's collection/Mapcraft.*

Solo commuters complained of trips taking twice as long. Ramp meters backed up traffic onto surface streets. Abrupt movements abounded as drivers transitioned from the fifty-five-mile-per-hour traffic in the Diamond Lane to a mixed-flow lane moving about five miles per hour. The average accident rate on the freeway jumped from two per day to twenty-five per day over the duration of the project.

On the following day, traffic conditions in the mixed-flow lanes improved only slightly. Complaints from drivers filled the op-ed pages of newspapers, blared over talk radio and clogged the Caltrans Diamond Lane telephone information line.

Some people thought Caltrans had a more sinister intent. They equated the Diamond Lane with socialism and communism. Comments such as, "We are seeing on the Santa Monica Freeway the beginning of the end of freedom of movement in the United States and the birth of a Soviet America," and "Those diamonds out there are Big Brother's heel marks, and they are beginning to look more and more like the hammer and sickle every day" filled newspaper op-ed pages.

Media coverage was mostly negative. During the months in which the Diamond Lanes were in effect, nearly every issue of the *Los Angeles Times*, the *Herald Examiner* and the *Santa Monica Outlook* featured articles with titles such as "Freeway Folly," "Dishonesty with Diamonds" and "Sin and the Diamond Lanes." Cartoonists, such as Paul Conrad of the *Los Angeles Times*, drew cartoons denouncing the project.

Local radio and television stations reported on the Diamond Lanes. While traffic reporters and disc jockeys made jokes about the traffic backups, television newscasters provided a platform for politicians and activists to present their opinions about the project. Articles about the Diamond Lane appeared in nationwide media outlets.

But Caltrans officials dug in. Donald Burns, head of the state Business and Transportation Agency overseeing Caltrans, said, "Now we expect a lot of howling from enraged motorists." He added, "Now we are prepared to suffer considerable public outcry in order to pry John Q. Public out of his car."

CITIZENS AGAINST THE DIAMOND LANE

The protest movement against the lanes started off small. Paint and nails were thrown in the Diamond Lanes, and people gave away "No Diamond Lane" bumper stickers at freeway on-ramps.

On March 29, 1976, attorney Eric Jubler filed a lawsuit in the California Superior Court, alleging that the Diamond Lanes had lacked the proper Environmental Impact Report. He also claimed the lanes violated several parts of the United States Constitution. The Pacific Legal Foundation, a Sacramento-based public advocacy legal organization, filed a similar suit in the United States District Court on April 9.

In early May, Randy Kirk formed Citizens Against the Diamond Lane (CADL). The group grew to about eighty members. "My phone hasn't stopped ringing since last Thursday with calls from people who want to join with us to end this project. We don't feel the bureaucracy has a right to impose its solutions on the people without their ever having a chance to approve these solutions at the ballot box." CADL protested against the lane as far away as Maryland, at one of Jerry Brown's presidential campaign appearances.

Anti–Diamond Lane protest on freeway. *UCLA Charles E. Young Department of Special Collections*, Los Angeles Times *Photographic Archives.*

Anti–Diamond Lane protest. *UCLA Charles E. Young Department of Special Collections*, Los Angeles Times *Photographic Archives.*

Anti–Diamond Lane protest at Brown campaign headquarters. *Los Angeles Public Library Photo Collection.*

CADL staged a novel protest on June 3. A mock funeral procession, complete with hearse, drove on the Diamond Lanes from Santa Monica to downtown Los Angeles, terminating at Jerry Brown's presidential campaign headquarters. Twenty protestors were cited for driving in the lane with fewer than three passengers.

Although the Diamond Lanes were not Gianturco's idea, she liked the concept and became a big proponent of them. In a July 21 interview, Gianturco reaffirmed her support for the Diamond Lanes. She said, "We believe that there is real merit to this kind of project. It's designed to do three kinds of things. One is to decrease air pollution, secondly conserve energy, and, third, do something about the terrible congestion problems we have. And it's supposed to increase carpools and bus riders, and it's done that. And, it's on those grounds that we think it's working; it's not that we are just out there doing something for the hell of it, essentially." By this time, Gianturco and the Diamond Lanes were inextricably linked in the minds of many Southern Californians.

CADL held another protest on August 2 at Caltrans headquarters in downtown Los Angeles. The protestors were dressed in cloth bandages to symbolize those injured in Diamond Lane–related accidents. They displayed a petition with four thousand signatures calling for the end of the Diamond Lane.

END OF THE LANE

On August 9, U.S. District Judge Matt Byrne ruled that Caltrans had implemented the Santa Monica Freeway Diamond Lane without filing the necessary environmental impact report. He ordered the project ended, and the lanes returned to general use, by August 13.

The next day, lone drivers swarmed into the Diamond Lane with a vengeance. The California Highway Patrol announced it would no longer enforce the three-people-per-vehicle rule. Traffic now flowed smoothly in all lanes.

In a televised debate with Los Angeles city councilman Zev Yaroslavsky, the Caltrans director conceded defeat. "We have lost this court suit," Gianturco said. But she continued, "We plan to appeal. We believe that on the merits of this project, it is the kind of way to go. The people of Los Angeles have demonstrated time and time again that they do not want to spend money for mass transit in any significant amounts," referring to a rapid transit sales tax measure that was voted down in June. "In the absence of preferential treatment and encouraging buses and carpools, I don't know where we go."

By mid-August, the Diamond Lane signs had been removed and the ramp meters reset to a less aggressive cycle. Only the diamonds painted on the freeway remained, to be sandblasted away within weeks.

SAN DIEGO FREEWAY DIAMOND LANE

While struggling with the Santa Monica Freeway project, Caltrans announced plans for another Diamond Lane on the San Diego Freeway

(I-405) between West Los Angeles and the San Fernando Valley. Unlike the Santa Monica Freeway project, which removed two lanes from general use, this Diamond Lane would be constructed from the northbound left-hand freeway shoulder. A southbound Diamond Lane would be added later.

Even though no existing lanes would be taken away, opposition to the project appeared immediately. After Yaroslavsky warned that the project would "back traffic clear up to the city of Beverly Hills," the council voted nine to one to sue Caltrans if the agency did not halt the Diamond Lane.

Gianturco said, "We have learned from the Santa Monica Freeway experience that we need more citizen participation. We didn't do enough of that and it backfired." She continued, "If that means delaying it, then we will. We need three or four months before moving ahead with the project." The City of Los Angeles dropped its plans to sue Caltrans when it learned the lane would not open until at least January 1, 1977.

On January 29, the lane opened to all drivers, not just carpools. Caltrans officials warned drivers not to use the southbound shoulder, which had not been opened as a traffic lane.

ADRIANA THE OUTSIDER

The nearly all-male cadre of highway engineers balked at the idea of a woman leading Caltrans, although few expressed their views publicly.

More infuriatingly, she was not an engineer, but a planner. What did she know about building highways? The engineers thought that they should be directed by someone who knew about building highways, not an "urban planner" more interested in carpool lanes, mass transit and other alternatives to roads. During the Diamond Lane project, one engineer groused, "Most of us wished we were back building freeways."

Gianturco was not known for a friendly disposition, whether dealing with engineers, legislators, other government officials or the general public. "She's quite articulate. But she can't say 'hello' without sneering," said Albert Rodda, a former state senator. Councilman Yaroslavsky noted, "She could have sold the Diamond Lane if she had educated the public rather than hitting them over the head with a hammer."

FREEWAY SLOWDOWN

During Gianturco's tenure as Caltrans director, freeway construction came to a near-standstill, as many projects were delayed, deferred or removed from the master plan. The Foothill Freeway (I-210) between La Verne and San Bernardino languished incomplete for decades. The Long Beach Freeway (I-710) segment through South Pasadena was never built. Although the real reasons were either lack of funds or local opposition, freeway supporters, both inside and outside of Caltrans, accused Gianturco of deliberately stalling the projects in order to force drivers to switch to public transportation.

The Century Freeway (I-105), linking Los Angeles International Airport and Norwalk, had been on the freeway master plan since at least 1956. Because it cut through poor and minority neighborhoods, residents of South Central Los Angeles, Willowbrook and Lynwood banded together and filed suit to stop construction. Court battles delayed the project for about a decade. By the time construction began in 1982, the proposed $100 million, ten-lane freeway had become a $2.2 billion project with six freeway lanes, two carpool lanes and light rail in the median. Residents also demanded and received replacement housing, job training and affirmative action programs to ensure that they were hired to build the freeway. The Century Freeway finally opened in October 1993.

In September 1976, the California Highway Commission, in a five-to-one vote, ordered Gianturco to start authorizing construction of additional freeways. She had been keeping about $309 million in reserve for maintaining the current freeway network. San Diego mayor Pete Wilson said, "We have to continue to finish off the freeway system. Perhaps [Jerry Brown and Gianturco] are deluding themselves by thinking that by not spending the freeway funds, they're going to be able to build some kind of a mass transit system."

California state assemblyman Walter Ingalls and state senator Alfred Alquist, both longtime critics of Gianturco, introduced legislation in 1977 that would remove some of Caltrans's authority. Their Assembly Bill 402 would replace the Highway Commission with a new California Transportation Commission. It would also create local transportation commissions, including the Los Angeles County Transportation Commission (LACTC). Most notably, the bill would transfer funding decisions from Caltrans to the legislature. Governor Brown signed AB 402 into law on September 28, 1977, over Gianturco's objections.

"GET GIANTURCO OUT!"

To her political enemies, it was not enough simply to undermine Gianturco's authority. They wanted her out. Shortly after the lane on the San Diego Freeway opened in January 1977, Assemblyman Paul Priolo said of Gianturco, "She's incompetent, she's arbitrary and dogmatic in the matter in which she handles things. Her background is at best questionable, her performance has been inept, and it's time to get rid of her. [Brown's] sense of loyalty to these people I think is distorted and he ought to wake up. Now's the time to get rid of Adriana."

In May 1979, the legislature voted on a budget for Caltrans, omitting Gianturco's $40,000 annual salary. The vote was merely symbolic, since she would be still paid from contingency funds or other sources.

The clamor for Gianturco's removal increased. In April 1981, Ralph Clark, chairman of the Orange County Board of Supervisors, called for a resolution asking Governor Brown to fire her. This action was spurred by a draft state transportation budget halving Orange County's transportation fund allocation. "This is Adriana Gianturco's version of highway robbery," said Clark. "I agree that we have to go to war and the best place to start is to ask for her resignation or for the governor to fire her." Alquist sponsored a bill requiring the Caltrans director be a licensed civil engineer. The bill did not pass.

AN OCCURRENCE AT TOWN CREEK BRIDGE

Gianturco and the highway engineers clashed over the Town Creek Bridge on California Highway 162 near Covelo, Mendocino County. Although the bridge carried a few vehicles per day, years of use by logging trucks had weakened the twenty-two-foot-wide bridge. Caltrans engineers recommended a new forty-foot-wide bridge, but Gianturco insisted that the new bridge be only thirty-two feet wide, costing $29,000 less. Two Caltrans officials, incensed that Gianturco, a non-engineer, was making decisions they felt should be made by highway engineers, resigned in protest.

In December 1981, California state senator Paul Carpenter, a particularly vehement adversary of Gianturco's, held a series of hearings about the bridge, as well as about whether Gianturco had the authority to specify its width.

He called Gianturco to speak at one of these hearings. Gianturco and her husband, John Saltonstall, were preparing to travel back to Massachusetts to visit family, and she asked the hearing to be postponed. Instead, Carpenter had a court issue Gianturco a subpoena.

Saltonstall went to the East Coast alone. While there, he was involved in a head-on auto collision. Defying the subpoena, Gianturco left to visit him in the hospital. Carpenter and others held the meeting in her absence. A few Caltrans engineers in the audience mocked her by saying things such as, "She got what she deserved."

The state Assembly Committee on Transportation, led by Assemblywoman Marian La Folette, began an investigation. Gianturco, citing the fact there had been no accidents on the bridge, asserted that she was legally allowed to make a decision on the width of the bridge. At the conclusion of the investigation in December, the state auditor general supported her authority regarding the bridge. A thirty-two-foot-wide bridge was built in 1994.

Public officials and the general populace alike ridiculed her, calling her "the ice-plant lady" (because of her interest in landscaping the freeways) and "Giant Turkey" (a play on her name). But Gianturco continued to defend her positions on freeway construction and mass transit. Although extensive development of a rail transit system in Los Angeles remained elusive (voters turned down a proposed tax to fund mass transit in June 1976), Caltrans funding expanded Amtrak service between Los Angeles and San Diego from three to five daily round trips. In October 1982, Caltrans funded a commuter train between Oxnard and Los Angeles. The train, heavily opposed by the Southern Pacific Railroad, failed to attract many passengers and was canceled in March 1983.

DEUKMEJIAN AND TROMBATORE

In November 1982, George Deukmejian was elected governor. Upon taking office in January 1983, he announced that he would direct additional funds to the highway system. In his State of the State speech, he said, "Our transportation infrastructure has badly deteriorated over the past eight years. My budget establishes priorities which shift the emphasis from exotic alternative transportation schemes over to the proven priorities of safe, well-maintained, and efficient highways." He replaced Gianturco as director of Caltrans by appointing Leo Trombatore, a highway engineer.

Under Trombatore, Caltrans built seven hundred miles of new freeways throughout the state. However, the big freeway-building boom of the '50s and '60s was a thing of the past. The anti-tax mood of the California populace had culminated in the adoption of Proposition 13 in June 1978, limiting available funding.

EPILOGUE

After leaving Caltrans, Gianturco spent most of her time lecturing at universities and transportation conferences, writing newspaper articles and caring for her elderly parents. She is currently serving on the board of directors of the Sacramento chapter of the ACLU.

Caltrans has had eight directors, including one woman, since Trombatore resigned in 1987. Although all struggled with changing transportation priorities and limited funds, none has been the lightning rod that was Gianturco.

When Jerry Brown became governor again on January 3, 2011, some speculated that he would reappoint Gianturco as director of Caltrans. But Malcolm Dougherty, a Caltrans veteran of more than twenty years, remained in the position.

At a transportation conference in 1994, Jerry Baxter, a Caltrans official, quipped that the Diamond Lane "may have set back HOV development in California ten years." While other parts of California, such as San Diego and San Francisco Bay Area, continued to develop and expand carpool lanes, development in Los Angeles and Orange Counties languished until 1985, when a carpool lane was added on the eastbound Artesia Freeway (SR-91). Unlike the 1976 project, this was an entirely new lane, created from the shoulder nearest the center median. Caltrans avoided the term "Diamond Lane" in its marketing materials, preferring to call the facility a "carpool lane" or an "HOV lane." Carpool lanes were shortly added to other freeways; by 2014, 950 miles of carpool lanes were available on Los Angeles County freeways.

Although there have been a few complaints from drivers unable or unwilling to carpool, most of the driving public seemed to accept the lanes because they were not created by taking a freeway lane from general use. When the Northridge Earthquake damaged the Santa Monica Freeway on January 17, 1994, Caltrans closed much of the usable part of the freeway to all traffic except buses and carpools, effectively reinstating the Diamond Lane with little opposition. Despite calls to make the carpool lane permanent, all lanes of the freeway were opened to general traffic when repairs were completed.

As of late 2012, HOV lanes on the Harbor (I-110) and San Bernardino (I-10) freeways are available to those who drive alone—for a price. The new Metro ExpressLanes allow access to single-occupant vehicles, equipped with transponders, for a fee. Carpools still use the lanes for free, although their vehicles now must also have transponders.

After her tumultuous directorship, Gianturco feels vindicated by renewed expansion of the carpool lane network and new rail transit systems that have developed since 1990. "All that stuff we talked about years ago is the stuff that's finally happening now," she said in a February 1994 *Los Angeles Times* article. "Carpool lanes, the Metrolink, the idea of using existing rail lines are all programs that we started way back then."

CHAPTER 13

THE FUTURE IS AN ABANDONED TUNNEL

The Los Angeles Downtown People Mover

Peple movers—or more formally, Automated Guideway Transit Systems—operate at nearly every large airport in the United States. These systems, using small automated, driverless vehicles on fixed guideways, efficiently shuttle passengers from terminal to terminal. West Virginia University in Morgantown, West Virginia; larger amusement parks; and a few shopping centers also sport people movers.

Interest in building people movers as public transit systems peaked in the 1970s but fizzled at the start of the 1980s. Los Angeles was chosen by the federal government as the site of one of these ultimately unsuccessful projects. However, the "ghost" of the project, the Bunker Hill Transit Tunnel, lives on, although it has been eclipsed by newer, more practical transit improvements.

THE FIRST PEOPLE MOVERS

The roots of the modern people mover were based in an exhibit at the 1964–65 World's Fair in New York. Ford Motor Company, seeking an efficient way to introduce customers to its products, hired Walt Disney to build what it called the "Magic Skyway." A fleet of Ford Mustangs was pushed along

Disneyland Peoplemover. *Los Angeles Public Library Photo Collection.*

a track by a series of spinning wheels. Speeds were slow enough to allow passengers to board a moving vehicle.

Disney used the basic principle of the Magic Skyway to build what was eventually named the "Peoplemover" at Disneyland in 1966. Small cars, each seating six passengers, were propelled along a three-quarter-mile-long guideway by five hundred spinning Goodyear tires. Top speed was about ten miles per hour, and the attraction could transport more than four thousand people per hour. Disney later built people movers, with different technology, at its theme park in Orlando, Florida, and at the Houston Airport.

PEOPLE MOVERS AND THE "GREAT SOCIETY"

When President Lyndon B. Johnson came into office in 1963, he signed into law a vast array of social welfare programs. On September 8, 1966, as he signed the Urban Mass Transportation Act, President Johnson declared, "In the next 40 years, we must completely renew our cities. The alternative is disaster. Gaping needs must be met in health, in education, in job opportunities, in housing. And not a single one of those needs can be fully met until we rebuild our mass transportation systems."

The act directed the secretary of housing and urban development to research improving existing urban transit, as well as new methods of providing transportation in cities. In 1968, the secretary's report, *Tomorrow's Transportation: New Systems for the Urban Future*, not only advocated upgrades to urban bus and rail systems but also called for research into new modes such as "personal rapid transit" (large networks of people movers covering entire cities).

Transpo '72

John Volpe, appointed secretary of transportation by President Nixon in 1969, was particularly interested in advanced transportation systems. To encourage the transportation industry, he set up a trade show in 1972 called Transpo '72.

Modeled on the famous aviation shows in Europe, Transpo '72 took place at Dulles Airport near Washington, D.C. About 1.25 million people visited the three-hundred-acre trade show between May 27 and June 4. Nearly every manufacturer of airplanes, helicopters, automobiles, trucks, boats, trains and mass transit vehicles exhibited their latest products. As both the Vietnam War and the Apollo space program were winding down, the federal government encouraged aerospace and defense contractors to build public transportation equipment.

The U.S. Department of Transportation provided funds for Bendix, Ford, Rohr and Otis Elevator to build test tracks and provide live demonstrations of their people movers. Westinghouse, Aerospace Corporation and other manufacturers exhibited static exhibits of their people mover cars. As attendees waited up to an hour for a short ride on the demonstration systems, UMTA officials hoped that the exhibits would encourage deployment of people movers, especially in urban transit settings.

LOS ANGELES CRA AND THE PEOPLE MOVER

The Los Angeles Community Redevelopment Authority (CRA), established by the state legislature in 1951, planned to redevelop Bunker Hill in downtown Los Angeles. In the 1960s, the CRA tore down the existing buildings and prepared to build skyscrapers on Bunker Hill. But because the streets would not be able to accommodate all who wished to drive and park, the CRA considered a people mover linking Bunker Hill with large parking structures on the outskirts of the central city. The project, which would feature a tunnel through Bunker Hill, would cost $58 million and open to the public in 1975.

Meanwhile, the City of Los Angeles implemented the Downtown Miniride, a circulator bus in the central city, on October 13, 1971. The city contracted with the Southern California Rapid Transit District (RTD) to operate the red-and-white minibuses every four minutes on a route serving most major downtown points of interest. After two months, daily ridership was about 3,100.

MAYOR BRADLEY IS INTERESTED

The people mover project gained an important ally in July 1973 when Tom Bradley was elected mayor of Los Angeles. One of his campaign promises was to improve public transportation.

By August, CRA had developed plans for an $82 million Auxiliary Transit and Satellite Parking System. This would be a 1.5-mile line connecting Bunker Hill with two satellite stations featuring parking. The people mover, while using aerial structures for most of its route, would run in a tunnel under Bunker Hill.

In September 1974, the Transportation Appropriations Subcommittee of the Senate Committee on Appropriations asked the Office of Technology Assessment to investigate the feasibility of people movers as public transit. OTA presented its report in May 1975. Although nine people movers served airports, theme parks and shopping centers, none had been built in a public transportation context. The report noted that the existing people movers were highly used and accepted, while warning, "The controlled environment of an airport or a recreation park is far different from an urban center, where passenger security, susceptibility to vandalism, and security of right of way are much greater problems."

UMTA, responding to the OTA report, announced a people mover demonstration program in April 1976. Cities were encouraged to apply for funds to build a people mover, although only a few would be chosen. The demonstration project was intended to test the usefulness of people movers in an urban transit context. In May, Mayor Bradley sent a "letter of interest" to UMTA, requesting that Los Angeles be chosen for one of the demonstration systems.

By July, a route had been selected. The people mover would link Union Station and the Convention Center via First Street, Hill Street, a tunnel roughly paralleling Third Street under Bunker Hill and then via Figueroa. Stations at Union Station and the Convention Center would feature four-thousand-car parking lots with direct ramps from the freeways.

Los Angeles was one of thirty-eight initial applicants. By October 1976, UMTA had cut the number down to nineteen. On December 22, UMTA announced its final selections: Los Angeles, Houston, Cleveland and St. Paul. Detroit and Miami, which had received earlier grants, were encouraged to continue working on their people movers.

UMTA allocated $125 million for transit in Los Angeles, with $100 million for the people mover. "This is a major breakthrough for our transportation program," said Mayor Bradley. "There's no doubt in my mind that this is a solid commitment from the Federal government to help with our transportation improvements. It's a giant step forward for Los Angeles."

In order to get the money, however, the city would have to formally apply for it. This required a vote of the city council, which voted nine to three to file the application on February 11, 1977. At about this time, CRA formed the Downtown People Mover Authority (DPMA) and appointed Daniel Townsend as executive director.

Federal support was somewhat uncertain. In May, President Jimmy Carter's new secretary of transportation, Brock Adams, expressed a preference for road and bus improvements rather than rail and people mover systems. A leaked memo from Carter himself showed his thoughts on recent rail transit projects in Atlanta, Baltimore and Washington. He called them "grossly overdesigned" and recommended cities implement simpler transportation improvements, such as off-street parking, one-way streets, bus lanes and surface rail systems.

As Los Angeles prepared to host the Olympic Games in 1984, people mover advocates hoped that the system would not only be operating but also be extended from the Convention Center to the Memorial Coliseum, a primary venue.

DOWNTOWN OR DISNEYLAND?

As the details of the people mover route were made public, opposition arose. Elevated structures along streets and sidewalks were no longer considered futuristic and progressive but rather ugly and obtrusive. Some complained that the structures would cast shadows, block views and take away parking and left-turn lanes. Others worried that the people mover would make

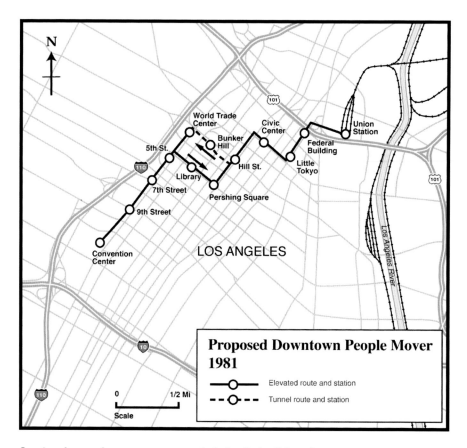

Los Angeles people mover route map. *Author's collection/Mapcraft.*

downtown Los Angeles resemble either Disneyland or the Chicago Loop with its elevated trains. In spite of the controversy, the city council voted, again nine to three, to start construction on March 27, 1979.

On May 9, the city council approved a modified route for the project. It was similar to the existing proposal, except that the Bunker Hill Transit Tunnel would carry one-way traffic; cars leaving Union Station and headed for the Convention Center would use the tunnel, while returning trips would use an elevated structure along Fifth Street, near the Central Library. Additionally, the Figueroa Street portion of the route would be shifted westward, toward the Harbor Freeway.

The Los Angeles Conservancy— a historical preservation organization concerned about the effect that the elevated people mover structures would have on the look of downtown Los Angeles—formed the group Taxpayers Revolt Against Needless Special Interest Transit (TRANSIT). This coalition knitted together interests as diverse as the San Fernando Valley, the NAACP, the Sierra Club and several transit advocacy groups. The League of Women Voters, while not part of TRANSIT, also expressed its opposition.

UTDC AND GAO

On August 19, 1980, Townsend announced that four companies had submitted bids to build the project: Matra Otis, Vought Corporation, Westinghouse and Urban Transportation Development Corporation (UTDC), a Canadian firm. Work had already started on the Bunker Hill Transit Tunnel, which consisted mostly of easements under buildings still under construction.

That same day, the U.S. General Accounting Office announced a critical report named *Better Justifications Needed for Automated People Mover Demonstration Projects*. The report claimed that instead of a demonstration of the value of people movers, the projects were added to the program for political reasons. The GAO also stated the need and cost effectiveness of the people movers had not been established by UMTA.

The other three cities originally selected by UMTA reconsidered their projects. Cleveland, under newly elected mayor Dennis Kucinich, discontinued its people mover and returned the funds to UMTA in 1977. Similar political changes led Houston and St. Paul to end their projects in

1979 and 1980, respectively. Work on people movers continued in Detroit, Miami and Jacksonville, Florida, using reallocated UMTA funds.

Voters elected President Ronald Reagan on November 4, 1980. In spite of the change in administration, Los Angeles pushed on with the people mover. On December 15, on the recommendation of DPMA staff, the city council voted to select lowest-bidding UTDC to build the people mover. Several officials expressed concern that UTDC had not yet built any working people movers; its technology only existed on a test track.

Criticism of the project continued. Councilman Bernardi said, "With 13 stations less than four blocks apart, a healthy frog probably could jump the distance from station to station and get there just as fast." Abraham Falick, of the Rapid Transit Coalition, referred to the proposed elevated trackage as a "Stonehenge of massive concrete pylons."

REAGAN AND THE PEOPLE MOVER

By this time, the attitude in Washington toward the people mover had definitely changed. President-elect Reagan formed a fifteen-member task force of transportation officials from the Nixon and Ford administrations. On December 15, the task force recommended deep cuts in federal support to transportation, particularly mass transit programs. The downtown people movers were especially singled out as being "worthless and politically motivated." Councilman Bernardi responded, "This is the first ray of hope that I have seen that this irresponsible project can be stopped."

Bradley warned that the people mover project would be in "trouble" without federal funds He urged the lame-duck Carter administration to fund the project. UMTA officials refused to commit to funding the people mover before Carter left office. "We've asked…for more information and until we get it we cannot proceed," said a UMTA spokesman.

The projected cost of the people mover had ballooned from $178 million to $250 million. To reduce costs, the DPMA unveiled a scaled-down project on January 15. Guideways would be narrower, two stations (Federal Building and Little Tokyo) would be consolidated into one (Los Angeles and Temple Streets) and the Ninth and Figueroa station would be deferred. Surface lots holding one thousand autos would replace the four-thousand-car parking structures at the Convention Center and Union Station. People mover stations would be simpler, without mezzanines or escalators.

By February, funding uncertainties made it unlikely the people mover would be completed at all. At a news conference in Los Angeles on February 10, Reagan's secretary of transportation Drew Lewis announced, "Any discretionary funds that are going to be available for new projects are going to be severely curtailed. And so I'm not going to be very encouraging in terms of having [the people mover] project finished, for example, for the Olympics."

"We've pushed all the right buttons. We've done all we can. It's in the hands of the gods now," remarked Councilwoman and project board chair Pat Russell.

PEOPLE MOVER DOOMED

On March 10, 1981, the U.S. Department of Transportation announced its budget: $1.6 billion in mass transit funding had been cut, including the $111 million for the people mover. Drew Lewis, alluding to the controversy over the system, said, "There is no sense in us getting involved in a local hassle over whether or not they truly want the system." About a month later, USDOT sent a telegram to DPMA, asking it to stop work on the project. Despite heavy lobbying by Bradley and other supporters, the House voted to delete the remaining $18.1 million of federal funds from the people mover on May 13. Daniel Townsend said, "I'm extremely disappointed. I think Los Angeles has lost its best chance of beginning mass transit in a decade."

In response to the federal cutback, the city council voted to end work on the people mover, develop a phase-out plan and dissolve the DPMA in June. "The project, as we know it, is dead," groused Townsend.

WHAT ABOUT THE TUNNEL?

However, included in the phase-out plan was $270,000 to study alternative uses for the nearly completed Bunker Hill Transit Tunnel. A small portion

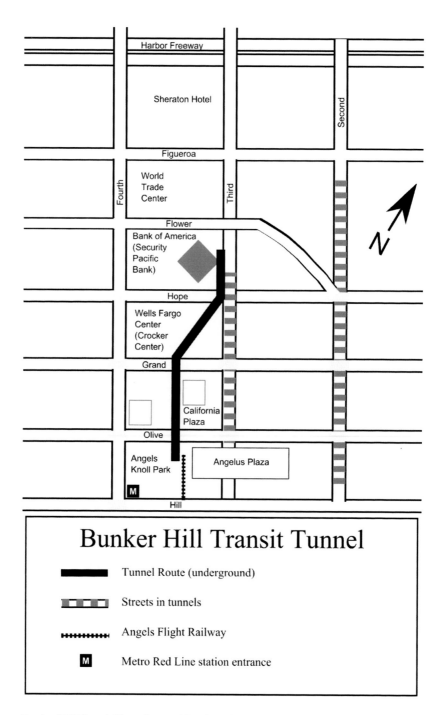

Bunker Hill Transit Tunnel map. *Map drawn by author.*

under Hill Street remained unexcavated. In December, CRA officials, noting that $15 million had already been spent on the project, suggested the tunnel be completed to accommodate a future, unspecified transit project. "There is no east–west access to Bunker Hill," said Townsend. "So we think it's important to go ahead and complete that small segment that is left."

Discussion of the Bunker Hill Transit Tunnel did not resume until 1986, when CRA announced plans to seek federal funding to complete a short section of tunnel under Olive Street. CRA officials still maintained that the tunnel might be useful for a yet-undetermined transit project.

UMTA offered an additional $3 million to complete the tunnel. A stipulation was that a transit project had to be in operation within one year after either Metro Rail or Plaza California Phase II, whichever came first, was completed. Otherwise, the city might have to return the money. The funding allowed the tunnel to be completed except for a small unexcavated section at Hill Street. (This was the site of the proposed, but never built, third phase of California Plaza.)

In 1990, the city commissioned a Bunker Hill Transit Tunnel study to determine possible transit uses for the tunnel. Since the tunnel was built for small vehicles and was only seventeen feet wide in places, a bidirectional light rail system through the tunnel would be impractical. After considering moving sidewalks, cable cars, electric buses, light and heavy rail transit and even magnetic levitation trains, the agencies concluded that a monorail, with cars small enough to fit inside the tunnel, would be the best use.

California Plaza II opened in 1992; the Metro Rail subway opened in February 1993. By the end of 1994, the city was no closer to running a transit system through the tunnel than it was in 1981.

On June 28, 2011, in response to state budgetary problems, Governor Jerry Brown signed Assembly Bill 26, which defunded and effectively dissolved community redevelopment agencies in California, including the Los Angeles CRA. Each agency would be allowed time to pay any outstanding debts and dispose of its real estate and other property. The easements composing the Bunker Hill Transit Tunnel will most likely revert to either the City of Los Angeles or to private owners sometime during or after 2015.

EPILOGUE

While the people mover and the Bunker Hill Transit Tunnel have faded from the public's memory, transportation options in central Los Angeles have improved tremendously.

The Los Angeles Department of Transportation (LADOT) took over RTD's Miniride shuttle in October 1985. LADOT rebranded it as DASH (Downtown Area Short Hop) and expanded it into a five-route network, carrying more than twenty-five thousand daily passengers.

Unlike the people mover, the Metro Red Line subway received federal funding. Construction began in 1986. On January 30, 1993, its first segment opened to the public, linking Union Station with the Civic Center, Pershing Square, the Financial District and the Westlake district just outside of downtown.

In March 2014, federal funding was approved for the Regional Connector, downtown's second subway. Designed to allow passengers easy transfers among the Metro Blue, Gold and Expo Lines, it will also enhance central city mobility with three new stations by 2020.

Downtown politicians and business owners support a proposed streetcar connecting the Broadway shopping corridor with the LA Live/Staples Center entertainment district, and possibly Bunker Hill. The City of Los Angeles has applied for federal transit funds for construction.

Angels Flight, downtown's "original" people mover, returned to service in 1996 after twenty-eight years in storage. Unfortunately, a fatal accident put the little railway out of service in 2001. Angels Flight returned to the rails in 2010, but safety problems sidelined it again in 2013. Hopefully, Angels Flight will reopen in the near future.

A people mover may yet come to Los Angeles, but not to downtown. Metro broke ground on its Crenshaw light rail line in January 2014. Since this line will pass Los Angeles International Airport (LAX), advocates are demanding stations in or near the airport terminals. To avoid expensive tunneling, airport and Metro officials plan to build a people mover connecting the light rail with the terminals. The people mover would also serve remote parking lots, car rental agencies and, in the future, could be expanded to serve airport hotels, reducing automobile and shuttle bus traffic around LAX.

CHAPTER 14

MOVING TOWARD METROLINK

The Oxnard—Los Angeles CalTrain

S ince October 1992, Metrolink commuter trains have operated throughout Southern California. Each weekday, nearly forty-four thousand passengers board trains at one of the system's fifty-five stations and enjoy a traffic-free commute to work, to school or for pleasure travel.

The path to Metrolink, however, has been rough. While Southern California has always had plenty of railroad tracks, efforts to develop commuter rail met with resistance and hostility from both railroad companies and certain politicians until the early 1990s.

THE FIRST COMMUTER RAILROADS

As railroads connected cities across the United States in the late nineteenth and early twentieth centuries, an important market was short-distance passenger trips between a large city and its suburbs. The railroads, to avoid overcrowding on the long-distance routes, offered additional trains called commuted ("cut short") trains. Passengers who rode them became known as "commuters."

However, in Southern California, because Pacific Electric's Red Cars performed most of this function, the mainline railroads provided few trips specifically for commuters.

After World War II, the railroads, facing competition from automobiles and airlines, discontinued passenger trains by the hundreds and focused on their highly profitable freight business.

By the early 1970s, concerns about the nation's disappearing passenger trains led the U.S. government to create the National Rail Passenger Corporation (Amtrak), to preserve and operate what was left of the nation's passenger rail network. However, the law that formed Amtrak prohibited it from operating commuter service. Local jurisdictions had to contract with the railroads in order to preserve commuter trains.

BAXTER WARD

As Southern California entered the 1970s, traffic congestion, air pollution and gasoline shortages heightened interest in commuter rail. In November 1972, voters elected Baxter Ward, a television news commentator, to the Los Angeles County Board of Supervisors.

A longtime train enthusiast and public transit advocate, Ward felt strongly that a rail transit system in Southern California would lessen traffic congestion, reduce air pollution and prepare the region for gasoline shortages. Primarily interested in a rapid transit system with its own right-of-ways, he also supported passenger trains using existing trackage to carry commuters from the suburbs into downtown Los Angeles.

Southern Pacific, Union Pacific and Santa Fe, the major railroads owning most of the trackage in Southern California, were not supportive of commuter trains. Fearing interference to their lucrative freight business, they vigorously resisted any passenger train service other than the Amtrak trains they were legally required to accommodate.

In 1973, the Southern California Association of Governments (SCAG) commissioned a study recommending two commuter rail trips between Oxnard and Los Angeles. In December 1974, the County of Los Angeles filed a request with the California Public Utilities Commission (CPUC) to enable commuter trains to use the Southern Pacific Coast Mainline across the San Fernando Valley and into Ventura County.

This was a single-track railroad with several sidings, requiring trains going in opposite directions be carefully scheduled. Amtrak's daily *Coast Starlight* was the sole passenger train. Major industries served included General

Baxter Ward. *Terry Guy photo collection.*

Motors and Anheuser-Busch in Van Nuys, Lockheed in Burbank and several lumberyards and other businesses. Southern Pacific and representatives of the businesses along the rail line expressed concerns about the disruption to freight service the commuter trains would supposedly cause.

BAXTER WARD'S "CHOO CHOO"

Despite the railroads' resistance and the opposition of fellow supervisors Peter Schabarum and James Hayes, Ward convinced supervisors Kenneth Hahn and Edward Edelman to vote to acquire eight 1940s-era passenger rail cars from an Oregon tourist railroad. On a three-to-two vote, the board of supervisors allocated $230,000 to purchase the cars and $1.8 million to refurbish them.

Ward named the train "El Camino" and planned to use it for commuter service on the Santa Fe Railroad between Orange County and Los Angeles Union Station. Unlike the three existing Amtrak round trips, the El Camino's schedule would be convenient for people working in downtown Los Angeles.

Santa Fe was unwilling to operate the El Camino or provide any support. While Amtrak was willing to run the train, it still was legally prohibited from running trips specifically for commuters. Amtrak agreed to operate the train as an additional Los Angeles–San Diego run, on a six-month trial basis. Los Angeles County and the California Department of Transportation (Caltrans) provided funding. No commuter-specific features, such as reduced fares or monthly passes, would be offered.

Schabarum and Hayes, along with other Los Angeles County officials, remained unimpressed with the idea, citing the millions already "wasted" on an antiquated train that had not moved in years. They called the train "Baxter Ward's Choo-Choo," "Baxter's Folly" and the "Train to Nowhere." But Ward insisted that the El Camino would run at least 80 percent full.

The first train left San Diego on February 14, 1978. Ward and Caltrans director Adriana Gianturco were on board. Each station featured a festive opening day ceremony. Various government officials, including Governor Jerry Brown, made speeches and then boarded the train. About three hundred passengers rode the El Camino into Los Angeles.

Regular ridership, however, only totaled about one hundred. Four significant problems existed. Upon arrival in Los Angeles, most passengers were some distance away from their jobs, requiring a bus or taxi ride. Many commuters found the El Camino's return run at 4:30 p.m. too early and used Amtrak's regular 5:30 p.m. trip instead, reducing El Camino ridership. The trains often ran late. Ward accused Santa Fe of "sabotaging" the commuter service by scheduling track construction projects. Santa Fe and Amtrak countered that bad weather, which damaged the tracks, was ultimately to blame for poor on-time performance.

August 12 marked the end of the trial but not the train. Amtrak, with financial support from Caltrans, added a new *San Diegan* train, using Amtrak equipment, on El Camino's former schedule. This marked the beginning of Amtrak and Caltrans working together to provide additional service on what would eventually become Amtrak's second-busiest route.

STRANDED IN SIMI VALLEY

The city of Simi Valley, on the Southern Pacific mainline to Ventura, was another supporter of commuter rail. During the 1970s, its population had grown from seven thousand to seventy thousand residents. The Simi Valley Freeway (SR-118) was still incomplete, so residents used surface streets to reach the San Fernando Valley and Los Angeles. "We're stranded. We don't have a freeway straight through. Yet seventy-five percent of our workforce commutes to Los Angeles," remarked Mike Sedell, an assistant to the city manager.

At an August 1979 CPUC hearing, after Southern Pacific representatives expressed their opposition to the commuter rail, Ward responded that the railroad was "psychologically against" passenger trains. "You cannot tell me that a railroad cannot schedule two trains in and two trains out without blowing up the San Fernando Valley," he said.

On June 4, 1980, CPUC ordered Southern Pacific to provide the commuter rail service. But in response to Southern Pacific's concerns, CPUC agreed in September to hear more testimony regarding commuter strain scheduling and interference with freight.

ANTONOVICH TAKES OVER

In late 1980, former state assemblyman Michael Antonovich, who opposed both the El Camino and the Oxnard–Los Angeles commuter rail projects, ran against Ward. During his campaign, Antonovich's television commercials showed a toy train and mocked Ward's "Train to Nowhere." On November 4, Antonovich won the supervisor's seat.

In his last days in office, Ward, by making an agreement with Caltrans to use the train on the Oxnard commuter service, temporarily prevented the county from disposing of it. However, once Antonovich assumed power, he, along with Schabarum and newly elected supervisor Deane Dana, rescinded the agreement. The El Camino remained in storage until 1985, when a tourist railway paid $365,000 and moved it to Mexico for use in Copper Canyon.

The new board of supervisors withdrew funding from the Oxnard–Los Angeles project, leaving only Caltrans and Simi Valley in support. "I don't know why L.A. County opposes it. L.A. can't possibly want Simi Valley's traffic on its streets any more than our traffic wants to be there," remarked Simi Valley mayor Elton Gallegly.

SP and CPUC

The battle between Southern Pacific and Caltrans continued in the courts. When a lower court refused to overturn CPUC's decision, Southern Pacific appealed the decision to the California Supreme Court, only to lose again in December 1980. On April 7, 1981, CPUC reaffirmed its previous order for Southern Pacific to start commuter train operations and called for both Caltrans and Southern Pacific to execute a contract for the service within 180 days.

Finally, in June 1982, CPUC ordered Southern Pacific to start the service on October 18. The railroad was to immediately start building passenger facilities and setting fares and timetables.

The California Transportation Commission allocated $6 million in state transportation funds for the commuter rail service, with $100,000 available for immediate use. Caltrans called the new train "CalTrain," the same name given to the San Francisco–San Jose commuter rail when the state agency took over that service from Southern Pacific in 1980.

On opening day, three hundred passengers, mostly politicians, other city officials and railfans, boarded the first train. Only thirty-eight people were actual commuters. The train only stopped at Oxnard, Simi Valley, Van Nuys and Glendale; other stations were not yet ready. The Oxnard station had no parking, advertising and marketing were minimal and the first train was delayed so that Caltrans director Adriana Gianturco could christen it with a bottle of champagne.

But she was confident that the low inaugural ridership was only a minor setback. "Even we didn't know for sure that the train was going to run until the last minute. That hurt us because people don't plan on using public transportation unless they know what they are getting. In addition to that, of course, any new service takes time to build up a ridership. People just aren't used to it yet."

The passengers seemed happy on board. "I'd rather ride this than drive any day," said one commuter from Oxnard. Another quipped, "Let's thumb our noses at those poor guys on the freeway" as the train passed near a crowded road. Some passengers griped about the fares (eleven dollars round trip from Oxnard); others complained about the lack of connecting bus service. But most agreed that the train was a much nicer alternative to being stuck in freeway traffic or a transit bus making many stops on its way downtown.

Ridership increased as more people found out about CalTrain through advertisements but leveled off at about 300 per day, far below the 1,400 predicted by Caltrans. Once stations at Camarillo, Moorpark, Chatsworth,

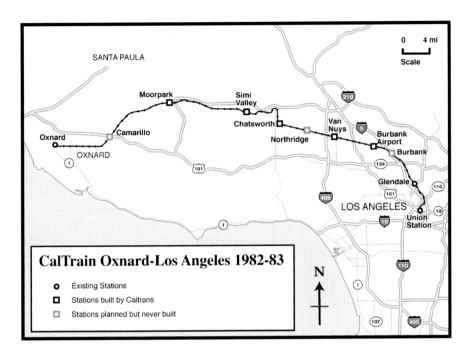

CalTrain map. *Author's collection/Mapcraft.*

Northridge, Burbank Airport and downtown Burbank opened, ridership would increase to 2,600, Caltrans officials promised.

CalTrain used Amtrak coaches until Amtrak needed them for the holiday travel season. Caltrans then borrowed several double-decker commuter cars from Chicago's Regional Transportation Agency (RTA). These cars also allowed faster passenger loading and unloading.

DEUKMEJIAN AND DERAILMENT

On November 7, 1982, California voters elected George Deukmejian as governor. Deukmejian regarded commuter rail as an "exotic" mode of transportation and promised to redirect transportation funding to highways.

On November 26, debris on the track punctured a locomotive's fuel tank as it was returning from Los Angeles. The train limped to Simi Valley, where passengers boarded Oxnard-bound buses.

This page: Caltrain. *Terry Guy photo collection.*

That same day, Southern Pacific announced that it was idling all General Electric P30 locomotives, including CalTrain's, because one had derailed in Texas. The railroad offered General Motors GP9 locomotives as replacements. Since these were incompatible with the RTA cars, Caltrans returned that equipment to Chicago and obtained compatible cars from the Bay Area CalTrain. However, the maintenance personnel in Los Angeles were unfamiliar with the CalTrain cars, requiring them to be sent back to

San Francisco for any major maintenance. Also, the cars' air-conditioning systems, designed for the Bay Area's mild weather, performed poorly in Southern California's warmer temperatures. Trains often ran with as few as one or two cars.

Although Gianturco, a Brown appointee, knew that her days were numbered under Deukmejian, her enthusiasm for CalTrain was unabated. She presided over the opening of the Chatsworth CalTrain station on December 29. As Amtrak's *Coast Starlight* thundered by, she stated, "[CalTrain] is doing exceptionally well, and its future looks bright. The fact that this service has shown a steady growth in ridership—doubling since late October—is a positive omen for its future success." In fact, the ridership had not doubled; it had only risen by 50 percent, still far below Caltrans's original predictions.

Once in office, Deukmejian kept his promise and zeroed out CalTrain from the state budget. Without funding, CalTrain service would end on June 30, 1983. In addition, Southern Pacific claimed that it was entitled to $588,000 per month to operate the trains; Caltrans was willing to pay only $70,000. Because of uncertain funding, Caltrans scrapped plans for stations at Northridge, Camarillo and Burbank; Burbank Airport and Moorpark stations opened in mid-January.

KREBS: TAXIS ARE CHEAPER

On Friday, February 4, passengers boarding CalTrain at Union Station received a flyer announcing that Southern Pacific was immediately discontinuing the commuter service. In a press release issued that day, Southern Pacific president Robert D. Krebs stated, "This experiment has been bad for the taxpayers of California, bad for the industries served along our line, and bad for Southern Pacific. While each individual commuter pays only a few dollars per round trip, the state's taxpayers are contributing about $170 for each commuter each day." He concluded, "It would be far cheaper for the State to give each CalTrain commuter a brand new car or a taxi ride to and from work each day absolutely free."

The next Monday, a federal judge issued a temporary restraining order forcing the railroad to resume CalTrain and purchase newspaper advertisements stating that the service had restarted. The trains, which had been moved to San Francisco for maintenance, rolled again on Wednesday.

On February 11, CPUC subpoenaed Krebs and several Southern Pacific officials, ordering them to attend contempt-of-Commission proceedings against the railroad. Southern Pacific officials insisted that the Staggers Rail Act of 1980 ended CPUC jurisdiction over railroads providing interstate service. The Commission fined Southern Pacific $16,000—$2,000 for each train that did not run on February 7 and 8. "We wanted to put [Southern Pacific] on notice that it can't decide on its own when it will or will not run a service," said CPUC executive director Joseph Bodovitz.

THE END OF CALTRAIN

Although riders expressed their support, CalTrain was losing friends in Sacramento. On February 15, Caltrans called for a temporary suspension of CalTrain until the subsidy dispute could be settled. About a week later, the California Transportation Commission (CTC) voted to recommend the legislature stop funding CalTrain, due to the low ridership and poor timekeeping.

Train supporters criticized Governor Deukmejian for not properly supporting CalTrain, calling to attention a $12,200 donation by Southern Pacific to his 1982 gubernatorial campaign.

During a series of CPUC hearings in late February, Warren Weber, Caltrans's director of rail projects, described Southern Pacific's operation of CalTrain as a "carnival road show." He continued, "If I were a commuter, I wouldn't buy a monthly pass because I don't know if it will run tomorrow," and he criticized Southern Pacific for late trains and non-uniformed conductors.

Nature's voice was heard when a powerful storm on March 2 washed away a railroad bridge near Moorpark. All rail service was halted until the bridge was repaired several days later.

Finally, on March 11, CPUC voted to suspend CalTrain indefinitely, while requiring Southern Pacific to retain the passenger facilities Caltrans had already built, in case service restarted. Although Caltrans officials thought that CalTrain might roll again one day, other supporters were not so sure. Douglas Ring, a former legal assistant to Baxter Ward, stated, "I do not see it being reinstituted under the [Deukmejian] administration, even if the tariff question is resolved. The administration came out against the train the day after [Deukmejian] was inaugurated, and I can only presume they made that decision without evaluating the service." On September 29, the

U.S. Ninth Circuit Court of Appeals reaffirmed CPUC's jurisdiction over Southern Pacific.

In April 1985, the Interstate Commerce Commission ruled that Southern Pacific could determine the cost of running CalTrain; since the railroad desired much more than Caltrans wanted to pay, the CalTrain service never resumed. By September, Caltrans and Southern Pacific had arrived at a settlement for past costs, including lease payments for stations built on rights-of-way.

MOVING TOWARD METROLINK

Although CalTrain was officially dead, commuter rail remained alive in the minds of transit officials. In September 1987, California state senator Alan Robbins, along with officials from Burbank and Simi Valley, advocated commuter rail through the San Fernando Valley be provided during an upcoming, four-year-long construction project on the Ventura Freeway.

By 1990, Amtrak's San *Diegan*, with support from Caltrans, provided eight daily round trips between San Diego and Los Angeles, plus two round trips to Santa Barbara. The earliest northbound train arrived at Los Angeles by 7:55 a.m.—early enough for commuters whose workday started around 8:30 or 9:00 a.m. A cadre of commuters, mostly higher-paid employees who could afford fares totaling $352 per month, rode this train to work each day. Changes in the laws governing Amtrak allowed it to operate locally funded commuter trains. In May 1990, Orange County paid Amtrak to operate the "Orange County Commuter," one additional round trip between San Juan Capistrano in Los Angeles. This train arrived in Los Angeles at 7:30 a.m., leaving workers plenty of time to take buses or shuttles to their jobs. Fares were also lower than on regular San Diegan trains.

Commuter rail planning remained a county-by-county effort until several key events in 1990. Former rail transit opponent Governor Deukmejian signed State Senate Bill 1402 in May 1990. This bill directed the transportation commissions of Los Angeles, Orange, Riverside, San Bernardino and Ventura Counties to develop a unified commuter rail plan. Southern Pacific, another former nemesis of commuter rail, sold 177 miles of right-of-way to the Los Angeles County Transportation Commission (LACTC). Santa Fe and Union Pacific also sold certain stretches of track and provided access

Metrolink train. *Author's collection.*

rights to others. Statewide transportation bond measures and countywide half-cent sales taxes approved by voters funded track improvements, new stations and rolling stock.

In response to SB 1402, the transportation commissions formed the Southern California Regional Rail Authority, or Metrolink, in June 1991. When the first Metrolink trains rolled from Pomona, Santa Clarita and Moorpark into Los Angeles Union Station on October 26, 1992, five thousand people boarded for fare-free rides that day. In 1993, Metrolink extended service to Riverside and San Bernardino and replaced the Orange County Commuter's single round trip with three.

After the January 17, 1994 Northridge Earthquake damaged several Southern California freeways, Metrolink, using federal emergency funds, extended service to the Antelope Valley and Camarillo. Ridership, which was normally about 9,500 daily boardings, spiked to 31,000, with the line to Lancaster alone carrying 22,000 daily boardings. Ridership dropped as the freeways reopened but has increased to about 40,000 as of 2014.

Metrolink has experienced serious problems. Passengers have complained of high fares (Metrolink fares are generally two to three times higher than the corresponding express bus fare), while taxpayer groups have complained of high subsidies (about 40 percent of revenues come from fares, with local transportation funds covering the remainder). And several accidents, including multi-fatality collisions in Glendale in 2005 and Chatsworth in 2008, have raised serious concerns about the system's safety.

But Metrolink has responded by developing new coaches with safety features and endeavoring to keep fares as low as possible, ensuring that commuter rail will remain a permanent fixture of Southern California's transportation landscape.

CHAPTER 15

JUMP IN THE BUSPOOL

Mac Barnes's Ground Link

Before dawn on October 10, 1988, several sleepy passengers shuffled onto a bus in Redlands, California. But this was not a Southern California Rapid Transit District (RTD) bus. Nor was it a Greyhound. This was Ground Link, a commuter buspool owned and driven by Mac Barnes, a vice-president at First Interstate Bank in downtown Los Angeles.

After everyone boarded, Barnes shut the door and maneuvered the bus out of the park-and-ride lot and onto Interstate 10. A couple of workaholics pulled papers from briefcases and started working, but the majority of passengers, some of whom had driven from as far away as Banning (twenty-two miles), quickly fell asleep.

Barnes continued along the freeway, pulling off to board more passengers in San Bernardino and Ontario. At Pomona, the last stop before Los Angeles, the sun was just rising as the last few riders straggled aboard. Back on the freeway, Barnes merged the forty-foot coach into heavy traffic. Nearing El Monte, he moved left into the busway, allowing the bus to zip past the near-standstill traffic in the mixed-flow lanes.

Unbeknownst to Barnes, an RTD driver saw the bus. Noticing that the bus lacked the certificate numbers required by law, he reported it to his supervisors, who in turn contacted the California Public Utilities Commission (CPUC).

The bus reached downtown Los Angeles at about 7:00 a.m. Unlike a fixed public transit route, Barnes occasionally varied his route in the central city, enabling his passengers to be dropped off as close to their jobs as possible.

After the last passenger disembarked, Barnes parked the bus in a lot near the First Interstate Bank building and walked to work.

The return trip home was much livelier. Passengers chatted among themselves, played cards at two tables near the back of the bus, watched videos or enjoyed wine and cheese brought on by another passenger. Everyone aboard was glad that they did not have to drive home in afternoon traffic.

About five months later, Barnes received a letter from CPUC. In the letter, he was charged with operating an illegal bus line and ordered to stand trial on April 5. Such an offense could bring a fine of $1,000 or even six months in jail.

MAC BARNES FORMS A BUSPOOL

Pliny MacNaughton ("Mac") Barnes Jr. was born on March 23, 1939, to electrical engineer Pliny M. Barnes Sr. and Ruth Barnes. The family lived in Mid-City Los Angeles, about eight miles west of downtown.

Barnes joined the U.S. Air Force in 1957 and served in Vietnam until 1965. Upon leaving the military, he enrolled at Mount San Antonio College, graduating in 1969 with an associate's degree in business data processing. He

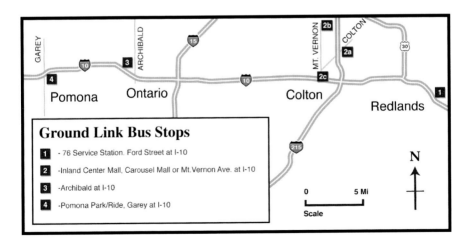

Barnes's Ground Link route map. *Author's collection/Mapcraft.*

made his career in banking, moving to Redlands in 1971 to supervise United California Bank's branches in Riverside and San Bernardino Counties. (United California Bank became First Interstate Bank in 1981.)

In 1975, Barnes was promoted to vice-president of the bank's compliance department, necessitating a sixty-four-mile (one-way) commute to Los Angeles. He and a few coworkers began a carpool. Other coworkers were also interested in sharing the ride, and by 1978, Barnes had bought a seven-passenger van due to increasing demand. Again, interest in ridesharing overwhelmed the van's capacity, so Barnes upgraded to a twelve-passenger vehicle and then a twenty-one-seat minibus in 1981. Finally, in 1982, he bought a forty-five-seat tour bus and began driving it between Redlands and Los Angeles every workday. The name "Ground Link" was chosen by a vote of the passengers.

Although a few passengers found out about Barnes's bus through Commuter Computer or other official ridesharing services, most riders discovered it through word of mouth or by seeing the bus on the road and calling the phone number emblazoned on the back.

BUSPOOL BACKGROUND

Starting in the 1970s, carpooling became a popular way of reducing traffic congestion and pollution, as well as providing a less stressful commute. Vanpools, or carpools using a van carrying up to fifteen passengers, were also common.

But the pinnacle of ridesharing was the buspool. Private bus companies, sometimes sponsored by major employers or community groups, provided daily service between a suburban park-and-ride lot and the workplace. This practice was especially common with aerospace firms in El Segundo, the San Fernando Valley and Orange County. The Greyhound-style coaches usually used for buspooling were much more comfortable than a public transit bus.

Rather than riding with strangers, passengers had the company of their co-workers. They could relax, nap or catch up on work on the inbound trip. On the trip home, the bus might resemble a railroad "club car," as passengers socialized, played cards and enjoyed snacks or even alcoholic beverages, which were illegal in carpools or vanpools.

In 1983, there were at least 132 buspool routes, operated by fourteen companies. Large bus companies such as Commuter Bus Lines, Antelope Valley Bus or Com-Bus operated the most routes. All buspool operators were subject to CPUC regulations regarding fares and routes. Competition among bus companies was keen, and disputes often ended up in court.

The bus companies, along with CPUC, also kept an eye out for anyone who operated without proper certificates. Garlene Zappitelli bought a new fifteen-passenger van in 1974 and started carrying co-workers along a route operated by Southern California Commuter Services, a buspool company. Zappitelli charged a fare to recover the costs of the van, including insurance and depreciation. SCCS complained to CPUC, which declared Zappitelli's vanpool an illegal bus line and ordered her to stop operating it. CPUC then ruled that vanpools could not be operated for compensation for expenses greater than direct costs such as gasoline and should not carry more than nine (later fifteen) passengers.

BARNES'S BUS AND CPUC

CPUC required commercial bus operators to pay a $500 filing fee plus 1 percent of all collected fares. The agency exempted not-for-profit vanpools carrying no more than fifteen people, but all large buses were considered commercial and subject to the fees.

Barnes considered these fees outrageous. Since his bus was run on a not-for-profit basis, he thought he should be exempted. "I never intended it to be a money-making deal," he said. "It was at best a break-even proposition." Passenger fares just barely covered the expenses of financing, fueling and maintaining the bus. Barnes once had to borrow $6,000 to keep the bus rolling.

In spite of his upcoming court date, Barnes continued his Redlands–Los Angeles bus service. "I don't agree with the law as far as its application to people in ridesharing," Barnes said. "The problem is that I'm unique or the beginning of something that's unique." He continued, "If we wait for governments to take care of the [traffic] problem, nothing's going to happen."

Media attention came to Ground Link, as local newspaper, radio and television reporters made the long trek to Redlands and then rode back to Los Angeles with the commuters. Bill Keene of radio station KNX, a longtime friend of Barnes's, criticized CPUC in on-air editorials. At a time when everyone was trying to encourage ridesharing, Barnes was providing an excellent way to rideshare, and a state agency was threatening him with fines and jail. But CPUC stood firm. "We are enforcing the law as it is written," said George Kataoka, a CPUC compliance officer. Assistant Director Paul Trahan agreed: "Here we have a guy for any reason could plow into a school bus some day and then people would ask, 'Did he have PUC approval to operate that bus?'" Any changes in the law, barring action by the state legislature, would happen long after Barnes's trial, he noted.

Barnes vowed to continue operating, even if he had to pay the fees under protest. "I have no intention to abandon this buspool. I have people who look to me for transportation to work," he said.

POLITICAL ACTION

One day, a passerby noticed Barnes cleaning the bus. The passerby happened to be an aide to California state assemblyman Bill Leonard, who represented Redlands. When the aide told Leonard of Barnes's plight, the assemblyman introduced Assembly Bill 1063. "To form a car pool is commendable and should not be something that hauls one into court," said Leonard. "I get very upset when PUC bureaucrats go after someone trying to perform a service that we all say needs to be done."

The bill amended CPUC regulations, allowing not-for-profit buspools to operate under the same rules as vanpools and waiving the onerous fees. From then on, buspool operators would only need a bus drivers' license, regular safety inspections, insurance and a more affordable seventy-five-dollar filing fee.

The bill included an urgency clause: "In order to quickly respond to the need for larger capacity ridesharing vehicles and protect the public by imposing insurance and safety requirements on these vehicles, it is necessary that this act take effect immediately." Unless Governor George Deukmejian vetoed the bill, it would automatically become law in twelve days, before Barnes's court date, now moved to June 13. "It just really reaffirmed my faith in the system," Barnes said. "This is the way I've always been taught the system should work. We found a defective law, we brought it to the attention of the people in government, and they took the steps necessary to correct a defective law." Leonard hoped that the bill would encourage more buspools to form. "I believe there should be some major employers considering van pools who might see it more cost effective to finance a bus program," he said.

Deukmejian signed AB 1063 on May 31, 1988. That afternoon, while sitting in traffic on the trip home, Barnes received the good news via cellphone and relayed it to his passengers. "I've got some good news and some bad news," he announced. "The good news is that the governor just signed the bill. The bad news is that I forgot to bring the champagne." Cheers went up as passengers celebrated the end of the struggle with CPUC, which dismissed the charges against Barnes a few days later.

Life Aboard Ground Link

Barnes continued to make his newly legal trips between Redlands and Los Angeles. The media attention helped fill the bus, as well as the waiting list. Passengers described the bus as cleaner, more comfortable and faster than anything RTD had to offer.

On board, friendships formed, and riders treated one another like family. Passengers freely left pillows, blankets and other personal property aboard the bus during the day, knowing that their items would be waiting for them for the afternoon commute. A few romances blossomed; Barnes married Donna Ward, one of his passengers.

During each of his trips, Barnes, using the name "East Side Spy," called Bill Keene at radio station KNX and described the traffic conditions on the freeway. The station would then incorporate Barnes's findings in its traffic reports.

END OF THE ROAD

Barnes planned to keep the bus after he retired. He wanted to convert it into a mobile home and take a long road trip across the United States. However, the economy worsened in the early 1990s. Ridership declined as passengers lost their jobs. "We lost twelve people in one fell swoop because of layoffs," said Barnes. Another factor was Metrolink trains, which reached San Bernardino in 1993. Although more expensive (a monthly ticket cost $208, as compared to $132 for Barnes's bus), Metrolink offered more frequent service and was better known. By October 1994, Ground Link ridership had dropped to twenty riders.

In 1995, Barnes was laid off from First Interstate. He sold the bus to a Hawaiian tour company and bought two vans for his remaining passengers. Barnes's passengers, some of whom had been riding since he bought the bus in 1982, were sad to see it go. Used to spreading out across two seats, they were not looking forward to the less spacious vanpools. "[The bus] has been a very comfortable arrangement. Now we're going to have to be belted in," groused one passenger.

EPILOGUE

After leaving First Interstate, Barnes worked as a personal financial planner for about eight years. Today, he is a parish administrator at First Evangelical Lutheran Church in Redlands and manages the Inland Master Chorale, a singing group.

"We had a great time with the buspool, but all good things must come to an end at some point," he recollected in an interview with the author. Although disappointed that he was unable to keep the bus, he is more distressed that no one started additional buspools after the regulatory changes. "We had put so much effort into having the laws changed so anyone could do this. But nobody to my knowledge ever followed through with it."

At the time Barnes sold his bus, buspools were becoming less common. The end of the Cold War closed or consolidated many aerospace plants; the buspools serving them were no longer needed. The economic downturn of the 1990s also eroded buspool demand.

New transit agencies such as Metro Rail, Metrolink, Foothill Transit and Commuter Express attracted commuters who formerly shunned RTD buses. Corporate ridesharing efforts promoted carpools, vanpools and transit but did not encourage buspools.

However, buspools are returning. High-tech companies such as Google, Apple and Facebook provide buspools for their Bay Area employees. More than ten thousand people ride these buses daily. Perhaps the success of these Silicon Valley buspools will encourage buspools to return to Southern California.

CHAPTER 16

A FREEWAY RUNS THROUGH IT

Driving on the Los Angeles River

W hat's so silly about a bargain freeway?" groused California state assemblyman Richard Katz in a 1989 *Los Angeles Times* editorial.

The "bargain freeway" was the bed of the Los Angeles River, stretching fifty-one miles from Canoga Park to Long Beach and lined with concrete as a flood-control measure. Katz, noting that the river was dry for at least two hundred days of the year, proposed using it as a reversible carpool lane between the west San Fernando Valley and Los Angeles. New on-ramps would allow buses and carpools into the river to travel into downtown in the mornings and return to the Valley in the evenings. The portion of the river between downtown Los Angeles and Long Beach could be used for trucks hauling freight to the ports, reducing traffic on the Harbor (I-110) and Long Beach (I-710) Freeways.

But Katz was not the first to propose using the river as a freeway. Ever since the river was paved, various government officials have considered allowing automobiles (or other vehicles) to drive on the concrete-covered riverbed as a freeway alternative.

LA River History

Before European settlement, the river provided water for drinking and irrigation to the adjacent village of Yang-Na, Los Angeles's predecessor.

During Spanish and Mexican occupation, the village grew to become the pueblo, and later the city, of Los Angeles. Open ditches, called zanjas, distributed river water throughout the city.

As the city grew, it consumed more and more water from the river, reducing its flow to an intermittent trickle. Surrounding cities, lacking their own water rights, were annexed to the city of Los Angeles, increasing water demands. In 1913, the Los Angeles Aqueduct brought water from Lake Owens to a growing city. The river, as a supply of water, became less important.

But when it rained in Southern California, the river became a raging torrent. After an especially deadly flood in 1934, Los Angeles County, along with the United States Army Corps of Engineers, channelized the river by paving it with concrete. As the project ended in 1940, the Los Angeles River became a concrete-lined flood-control channel. Only a few small portions— namely the Sepulveda Basin, the Glendale Narrows (near Griffith Park) and the segment south of Willow Street in Long Beach—remained unpaved.

An oily trickle of treated wastewater and street runoff flowed along a so-called low-flow channel in the center of the riverbed, leaving the rest of the concrete bottom dry. The river was also a dumping ground for trash, abandoned shopping carts and the occasional junk car. Graffiti covered the concrete, and homeless people bathed in the dirty water.

ROLLING ON THE RIVER

Although the river was too shallow and its current too intermittent to carry any vessels larger than a kayak, it became an important transportation corridor. When the railroads came to Los Angeles, their tracks flanked the river's banks in and around the central city. Monorail proponents, from Joseph Fawkes in 1910 to those in the 1960s and '70s, considered using the riverbanks as a right-of-way. Transit officials considered the riverbank as an alternate route for the Metro Blue Line but decided to route the light rail via Long Beach Boulevard instead.

Proponents of road transportation were also attracted to the river. City planners John and Fredrick Olmsted (sons of the great landscape architect Fredrick Law Olmsted), along with Harland Bartholomew, proposed a "River Truck Speedway" along the riverbanks in 1924. About four years later, they proposed a beautification program for the Los Angeles River, with service roads along the riverbanks. The Depression, along with the prioritization of flood control, shelved these plans.

The paved riverbed, however, captured the imagination of motorists and transportation planners. In early 1941, Los Angeles County supervisor Gordon L. McDonough advocated using the riverbed as a freeway between Burbank and Long Beach. As World War II raged in Europe and Asia, McDonough particularly stressed the strategic value of such a roadway. The river passed near the Lockheed, Vega, Vultee and Douglas aircraft plants, and the roadway could feature bomb shelters and pavement capable of supporting fifty-ton military tanks. McDonough presented his proposal to the United States Senate Defense Investigating Committee and requested that it be included in any appropriation bill for strategic roads. Although Congress took no official action toward a river freeway, trucks carrying war materials sped along the riverbed to the harbor after the United States entered the war.

Interest in turning the river into a freeway increased after the war ended. Los Angeles County supervisor Raymond Darby hosted a driving tour of the riverbed in August 1947. He argued for a redesigned low-flow channel, 10 feet deep and 50 feet wide, that would leave about 170 feet for traffic lanes. In the flood season, the river freeway would be closed entirely. Darby was confident that engineers could determine how to keep drivers out of flood danger. "People in Duluth [Minnesota] don't disregard their harbor facilities just because they're frozen over a short part of the year," he remarked. But the Department of Highways continued building freeways alongside, not in, the river.

In July 1954, several commuters discovered an unlocked gate near San Fernando Road, allowing them to use the riverbed as a "poor man's freeway" between that point and downtown Los Angeles. Traffic officials quickly installed a roadblock, preventing any further use of this "shortcut." Drag racing on the riverbed was also popular, and the police routinely arrested "hot-rodders" by the hundreds.

"There Is Water in It"

In 1960, California state assemblyman John Collier, representing the Eagle Rock district of Los Angeles, was concerned about freeway construction displacing residents. He called for a study of the possible use of the paved beds of both the Los Angeles and Santa Ana Rivers as freeways. "These riverbeds are flooded only about seven or eight days a year and could be available for use during the remainder of the time," he said. As Katz would propose nearly forty years later, Collier envisioned a "reversible" freeway carrying traffic inbound to downtown in the morning and outbound in the evening.

At a meeting of the state Assembly Interim Committee on Transportation and Commerce, held on October 3, 1960, Collier spoke with passion about the need to use the riverbed for traffic. Emerson Rhymer, an attorney for the Department of Highways, responded that while the department had considered using riverbeds as freeways, there were "many, many problems involved." The river was not wide enough, certain curves in the river were too sharp and the disposal of treated sewage, as well as the rights of people downstream using the river water, had to be considered. Ramps would be needed to allow cars to travel in and out of the river; these ramps would have to be designed as to not impede water flow during a rainstorm. Rainy weather would obviously close a river freeway. The debris left behind after a storm would require time and money to remove. Rhymer presented a letter from the Army Corps of Engineers reiterating most of the points he made and discouraging the use of the river as a roadway. "Believe it or not, there is water in it," he said.

Collier continued to argue in favor of the river freeway and authored a resolution, asking the committee to study the feasibility of a riverbed freeway. The study, completed in January 1961, concluded that the idea of using the riverbed or flood-control channels as freeways posed "problems considered insurmountable." Opposition from the Department of Highways, the Army Corps of Engineers and the surrounding cities of Burbank, Glendale, Pasadena and South Pasadena put an end to Collier's river freeway dream.

River transportation ideas were not just limited to road and rail. Another county supervisor, Leonard J. Roach, proposed using the riverbed between First Street and Washington Boulevard as an airport runway. Although Roach tried to convince the city's Airport Commission that the river airport would "bring passengers within five minutes of the Biltmore [Hotel]," the commission chose to expand Mines Field (current-day Los Angeles International Airport) instead.

In 1964, Robert Paul, a retired Los Angeles Department of Water and Power engineer, advocated the use of hovercraft in the Los Angeles River and other paved waterways. Hovercraft were also mentioned in a 1979 Port of Los Angeles report.

FLOWING INTO THE '70S

By the early 1970s, most vehicular use of the river was limited to driver training for police officers and bus drivers. The river was also popular with filmmakers; movies such as *Grease* were filmed there.

The California Department of Transportation (Caltrans), facing political opposition to new freeways, considered using the wide portion of the river south of Los Angeles as a roadway. A 1972 study discussed building ramps to allow vehicles access to eighteen miles of the riverbed between Willow Street in Long Beach and the Golden State Freeway near downtown Los Angeles. Another study in 1976 proposed using the riverbed as a bus-only roadway between Imperial Highway and central Los Angeles. In 1979, Caltrans advocated a truck-only highway along the riverbed, connecting the Golden State Freeway with San Pedro.

On June 26, 1979, officials of RTD and Army Corps of Engineers representatives drove on the riverbed in a three-car caravan. At various points along the way, they encountered restricted vertical and side clearances, trash, dust, mud, debris and the occasional pedestrian. Bumps

RTD bus driver training in Los Angeles River. *UCLA Charles E. Young Department of Special Collections,* Los Angeles Times *Photographic Archives.*

in the pavement scraped the underside of the caravan's automobiles. RTD officials expressed concern that these bumps could cause a bus to "bottom out," disabling it. Both RTD and Corps officials concluded that extensive modifications would be required to make the riverbed suitable for use as a busway.

FREEWAY OR GREENWAY?

Twenty years passed between that exploration and Richard Katz's idea to put traffic lanes in the bed of the Los Angeles River.

Born on August 16, 1950, Katz spent all of his early life in Los Angeles. His family moved from the Griffith Park area to West Los Angeles and then finally to the San Fernando Valley.

He got his first taste of politics in 1971, when he ran for student body president at San Diego State University. After graduation, he attended law school for about a year. However, his real interest was politics, and he dropped out of school to participate in George McGovern's 1972 presidential campaign and George Moscone's 1973 campaign for governor.

In 1980, he was elected to the California State Assembly, representing Sylmar in the northeastern San Fernando Valley. Katz became known as a tenacious legislator, campaigning across the state for projects such as a toxic waste dump cleanup act in 1984. He was also very interested in transportation, and in 1985, Assembly Speaker Willie Brown appointed him as head of the influential Assembly Transportation Committee. Katz was a strong proponent of a magnetic levitation train between Anaheim and Las Vegas, and in 1989, he authored Proposition 111, a transportation-funding measure approved by voters in June 1990.

Katz predicted that the riverbed lanes would remove up to six thousand cars daily from the Ventura and Golden State Freeways. His proposal, estimated at $30 million, cost one-tenth the price of the Los Angeles–North Hollywood Metro Red Line, then under construction.

A few transportation officials offered guarded support. Jim Sims of the Los Angeles Department of Transportation (LADOT) said, "We're at the point that we may be running out of attractive alternatives. And we may be at the point where we could live with something we can't use all the time." Bill Keene, traffic reporter for radio station KNX, remarked, "It's great if

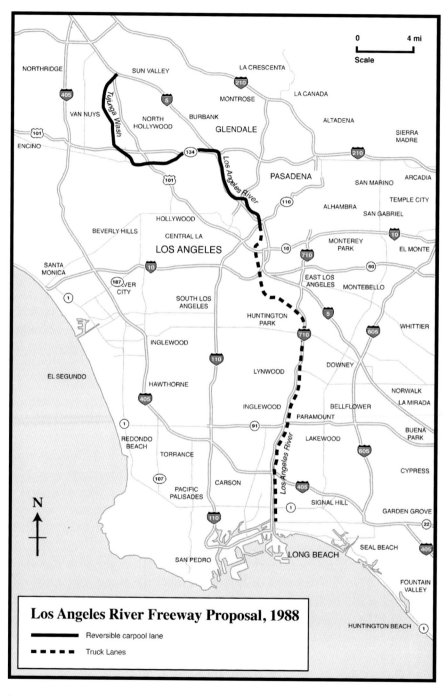

Los Angeles River Freeway proposal. *Author's collection/Mapcraft.*

the weather stays decent," and further suggested trucks use the waterways to prevent accidents on freeways.

Others found the idea questionable. Alan F. Pegg, general manager of RTD, wondered whether the river channel was wide enough to serve as both a roadway and a flood-control facility. "It's a very worthwhile corridor in many ways. But the technology has to be there to do it. I think that's somewhat in question."

The general public either considered the idea a joke or came out against it. "We are not going to accept a Mickey Mouse, Band-Aid solution to the problems of runaway growth," said Gerald Silver, leader of an Encino homeowners' group.

Mayor Tom Bradley, who was elected to what would be his final term in April 1989, made river restoration a campaign promise. Possibly inspired by several *Los Angeles Times* articles written by Dick Roraback, who explored the entire river in 1985, Bradley expressed his opposition to using the river for vehicular traffic. Deputy Mayor Mike Gage said, "We still think that it makes a lot more sense to use the river as a recreational and aesthetic resource. I don't want to discourage Mr. Katz from looking at alternatives but I honestly hope he'll see a need for open space and green space and not another noisy, polluting concrete freeway."

But Katz was undeterred. "As a less expensive answer to congestion, the riverbed should not be ignored," he said. "It just makes sense to look at it. It's just too good to pass up."

FRIENDS OF THE RIVER

"He'll build it over our dead bodies. The L.A. River is not a freeway," responded Lewis MacAdams, whose small but growing Friends of the Los Angeles River (FoLAR) had other ideas for the future of the waterway.

MacAdams, a Texas-born poet, writer and laborer, moved to Bolinas, thirty miles north of San Francisco, in 1970. There, he successfully fought an Army Corps of Engineers project that would have dumped treated sewage into the ocean. He also served on the local water board before coming to Los Angeles in 1980. While working on a building restoration project in downtown Los Angeles, he had his first glimpse of the concrete-lined river.

Flyer advertising one of FoLAR's river cleanup events. *Courtesy FoLAR.*

Opposite: Assemblyman Richard Katz promoting the river freeway. *Los Angeles Public Library Photo Collection.*

His explorations of the river, however, did not begin until mid-1985, when he, along with a few friends, cut through a chain link fence and walked along the riverbed. As freight trains rumbled overhead and traffic sounds from nearby highways echoed in the concrete channel, he decided that the river should be restored to its natural state. "We asked the river if we could speak for it in the human realm. We didn't hear it say no, and that was how Friends of the Los Angeles River began," recalled MacAdams.

In September 1985, FoLAR put on a short, avant-garde play dramatizing the flora and fauna of the river. Although panned in the press (one reviewer wrote, "With friends like these, the Los Angeles River doesn't need any enemies"), ticket proceeds provided initial funding for the group. As membership grew, FoLAR held river restoration activities such as trash cleanups and graffiti removal. These events were performed without permission from the Army Corps of Engineers or any other agency.

KATZ KORRIDOR

Meanwhile, Katz continued to promote his river freeway plan. On August 3, at a press conference on the bank of the river near Griffith Park, he presented several artists' drawings of the project. There would be three lanes of traffic, an improved low-flow channel to keep the traffic lanes as dry as possible and a greenbelt of trees and grass. Katz said, "Until now, the river has been wasted space. My proposal would take traffic off the streets and help the environment." MacAdams was not satisfied. "They're talking about paving the only living part of the river," he said, referring to the unpaved Glendale Narrows section. "Is the whole city going to be covered in concrete?"

On October 14, Katz demonstrated his support for the river freeway by driving along the river bottom after entering through an open gate near Glendale. "Only in L.A. would you think of putting cars into a riverbed. But only in L.A. would you have a riverbed in 18 inches of concrete. Mine may not be the total solution, but it is a solution. And I understand why people are skeptical of my idea. If it's so simple, they wonder why it hasn't been done already. That's what I'd like to know too." As he drove through puddles of treated sewage, he sped up through the wider portion of the river between LA and Long Beach. "Just look at this! Eight lanes! The infrastructure. It's all here!" he exclaimed.

Encouraged by Katz, and over the protests of FoLAR and other environmental groups, LACTC allocated $100,000 for study of the riverbed freeway on October 25.

Katz's river freeway became the butt of many jokes. On November 27, a *Los Angeles Times* editorial favoring river restoration was subtitled, "It No Longer Flows Only When It's Raining Katz and Dogs." *Los Angeles Daily News* humor columnist Dennis McCarthy wrote, "This year's 'Best Idea to Get Laughed At' award goes to Assemblyman Richard Katz and his proposed freeway in the Los Angeles River. Will the gentlemen from the Department of Transportation please control themselves or leave?"

In January 1990, as the winter rains filled the river, Mayor Bradley presented his park proposal. "The potential for the Los Angeles River as a recreational resource is enormous," said Bradley. "Along the banks, we can plant trees, build bicycle paths or create and enhance open-space areas. I'm very excited about the possibilities." Councilman Joel Wachs agreed: "The city has two choices: We can either pave over the river or turn it into a great natural resource. This decision will do more to shape the future of Los Angeles than anything else before us."

Governor George Deukmejian, on September 25, signed Senate Bill 1920, calling for the California Coastal Conservancy to develop a plan to restore the river and provide recreational activities. The bill was authored by

California state senator Art Torres, a leading proponent of river restoration. Katz, initially opposed because it made no plans for his riverbed freeway, eventually supported it hoping that a mass transit facility would be included in the conservancy's plan.

The LACTC presented its report on the river freeway proposal in February 1991. On March 20, 1991, the LACTC's Planning and Mobility Committee voted to put Katz's project on hold in order to give the Army Corps of Engineers and the Los Angeles County Flood Control District, both of which had opposed similar projects in the past, time to determine the environmental and flood-control impacts of the river freeway.

THE STORM OF 1992

A huge rainstorm swept across Southern California on February 11, 1992. The river became a raging torrent. At least one person fell into the river and was swept out to sea.

The next day, Los Angeles city councilman Michael Woo, along with MacAdams, held a press conference near the riverbank. As the waters rushed and swirled behind him, Woo remarked, "All I can say today is thank God we haven't turned the L.A. River into a freeway because, if we had, those motorists would have been in a lot of trouble…One thing is certain: This is no place for trucks and cars."

Katz continued to defend his proposal. "Freeways were flooded yesterday, and we are not talking about abandoning using freeways," Katz said in a telephone interview from Sacramento. "You have to shut down [Interstate 5 at] the Grapevine when it snows, but you don't restrict people from using it the rest of the year." Both he and Woo were now campaigning to become mayor, and Katz felt that Woo was using the flood for political purposes. "At a time when we're pulling people out of trees and off the tops of cars and digging out of the disaster, it's just unfortunate that people use times like this for cheap political shots," Katz said.

After the storm, the river freeway proposal disappeared from discussion at LACTC, while FoLAR and other river preservationists redoubled their efforts to restore the river to its natural state. On August 17, Senator Torres introduced Senate Bill 20, which would create a Los Angeles River Conservancy. While the bill contained elements of both Torres's and Katz's earlier bills, it made no provision for use of the riverbed by motor vehicles. Five days later, the California State Senate voted thirty-one to zero in favor of the bill. Torres remarked, "The Los Angeles River really has an opportunity to come to life again...Let us turn back the clock and have a real river again."

EPILOGUE

The passage of SB 20 in 1992 marked the end of a long series of plans to use the river as a roadway and the beginning of the restoration of the waterway. FoLAR, the Los Angeles River Conservancy and other river preservation groups, such as the Los Angeles River Revitalization Corporation (LARRC), continue to advocate for both preserving ecological habitats and providing recreational opportunities along the river.

However, even the staunchest opponent of the river freeway admitted that the idea of the river freeway played a part in the restoration efforts. "The Katz proposal really got people thinking about the river," said MacAdams in a 1997 interview with Blake Gumprecht, author of *The Los Angeles River: Its Life, Death and Possible Rebirth*. "I have often said that Richard Katz was one of the best friends the Los Angeles River ever had."

In July 2010, the U.S. Environmental Protection Agency designated the Los Angeles River a "navigable" body of water under the Federal Clean Water Act, affording the river certain protections. And in May 2013, the (unpaved) Glendale Narrows was officially opened for public recreation, such as kayaking. Several bicycle paths have been built alongside portions of the river; the LARRC has announced plans to improve existing paths and build new ones over the entire fifty-one-mile length of the river.

But perhaps the most surprising event was when the Army Corps of Engineers presented its *Los Angeles River Ecosystem Restoration Integrated Feasibility Report* in September 2013. This document discussed nineteen alternative plans for river restoration, including the removal of concrete from the riverbed. In May 2014, the Corps recommended an ambitious, $1 billion plan for restoring much of the river to its natural state. Everyone in favor of restoring the river, including MacAdams, accepts that it will be a long-term process. "When the yellow-billed cuckoo is singing in the sycamores, our work will be done," said MacAdams.

Katz, after leaving office in 1996 due to term limits, has continued his involvement in transportation through his appointments to the boards of the Los Angeles Metropolitan Transportation Authority (Metro), the Southern California Regional Rail Authority (Metrolink) and the Los Angeles City Planning Commission. However, he has been relatively silent about his river freeway proposal ever since. When questioned about it at a transit advocates' meeting in December 2008, he simply shook his head and grinned.

BIBLIOGRAPHY

BOOKS

Ayer, Bob. *History of Santa Monica's Big Blue Bus*. Santa Monica, CA: City of Santa Monica, 1984.

Bail, Eli. *From Railway to Freeway: Pacific Electric and the Motor Coach*. Glendale, CA: Interurban Press, 1984.

Barlett, Donald L., and James B. Steele. *Howard Hughes: His Life & Madness*. New York: W.W. Norton, 2004.

Black, Alan. *Urban Mass Transportation Planning*. New York: McGraw-Hill, 1995.

Borgeson, Griffith. *Errett Lobban Cord: His Empire, His Motorcars: Auburn, Cord, Duesenberg*. Princeton, NJ: Automobile Quarterly Publications, 1984.

Branch, Melville Campbell. *Urban Air Traffic and City Planning: Case Study of Los Angeles County*. New York: Praeger Publishers, 1973.

Brown, Lee, and Robert L. Allen. *Strong in the Struggle: My Life as a Black Labor Activist*. Lanham, MD: Rowman & Littlefield, 2001.

Brunner, Francis. *Southern California's Prettiest Drive: A Tour along the Crescent Shore of Santa Monica Bay and Up into the Picturesque Canyons of the Santa Monica Mountains*. N.p., 1925.

Cannato, Vincent J. *American Passage: The History of Ellis Island*. New York: Harper, 2009.

Comer, Virginia L. *Angels Flight: A History of Bunker Hill's Incline Railway*. Los Angeles: Historical Society of Southern California, 1996.

Crump, Spencer. *Ride the Big Red Cars: How Trolleys Helped Build Southern California*. Los Angeles: Crest Publications, 1962.

Duke, Donald. *Incline Railways of Los Angeles and Southern California*. San Marino, CA: Golden West Books, 1998.

Dwiggins, Don. *Hollywood Pilot: The Biography of Paul Mantz*. Garden City, NY: Doubleday, 1967.

Finson, Jon W. *The Voices that Are Gone: Themes in Nineteenth-Century American Popular Song*. New York: Oxford University Press, 1994.

Friedricks, William B. *Henry E. Huntington and the Creation of Southern California*. Columbus: Ohio State University Press, 1992.

Gifford, Jonathan Lewis. *Flexible Urban Transportation*. Amsterdam: Pergamon, 2003.

Gillingham, Robert C. *The Rancho San Pedro: The Story of a Famous Rancho in Los Angeles County and of Its Owners the Dominguez Family*. Los Angeles, 1961.

Giuliano, Genevieve, and Roger F. Teal. *Urban Transit: The Private Challenge to Public Transportation*. San Francisco, CA: Pacific Institute for Public Policy Research, 1985.

Gottlieb, Robert. *Reinventing Los Angeles: Nature and Community in the Global City*. Cambridge, MA: MIT Press, 2007.

Gumprecht, Blake. *The Los Angeles River: Its Life, Death, and Possible Rebirth*. Baltimore, MD: Johns Hopkins University Press, 1999.

Hichborn, Franklin. *Story of the Session of the California Legislature of 1915*. San Francisco: Press of the James H. Barry, 1916.

Hopkins, George E. "The Trouble with E.L. Cord." In *Flying the Line: The First Half Century of the Air Line Pilots Association*. Washington, D.C.: ALPA, 1982.

Horne, Gerald. *Fire This Time: The Watts Uprising and the 1960s*. New York: Da Capo Press, 1997.

Hubler, Richard Gibson. *Straight Up: The Story of Vertical Flight*. New York: Duell, Sloan and Pearce, 1961.

Lave, Charles A. *Urban Transit: The Private Challenge to Public Transportation*. San Francisco, CA: Pacific Institute for Public Policy Research, 1985.

Leterman, Elmer G., and Thomas W. Carlin. *They Dare to Be Different*. New York: Meredith Press, 1968.

Lotchin, Roger W. *Fortress California, 1910–1961: From Warfare to Welfare*. New York: Oxford University Press, 1992.

Ludwig, Ella A. *History of the Harbor District of Los Angeles, Dating from Its Earliest History*. Los Angeles, CA: Historic Record, 1927.

Mayers, Jackson. *Burbank History*. Burbank, CA: J.W. Anderson, 1975.

Meginness, John Franklin. *Biographical Annals of Lancaster County, Pennsylvania, Containing Biographical and Genealogical Sketches of Prominent and Representative Citizens and of Many of the Early Settlers*. Chicago: Beers, 1903.

Meissner, Loren P., and Kim Jarrell Johnson. *A Brief History of Eastvale*. Charleston, SC: The History Press, 2013.

O'Flaherty, Joseph S. *An End and a Beginning: The South Coast and Los Angeles, 1850–1887*. New York: Exposition Press, 1972.

Page, Henry Markham. *Pasadena: Its Early Years*. Los Angeles: privately printed by L.L. Morrison, 1964.

Rindge, Frederick Hastings. *Happy Days in Southern California*. Cambridge, MA, 1898.

Schwantes, Carlos A. *Going Places: Transportation Redefines the Twentieth-Century West*. Bloomington: Indiana University Press, 2003.

Sears, David O., and John B. McConahay. *The Politics of Violence: The New Urban Blacks and the Watts Riot*. Boston: Houghton Mifflin, 1973.

Seims, Charles. *Trolley Days in Pasadena*. San Marino, CA: Golden West Books, 1982.

Sides, Josh. *L.A. City Limits: African American Los Angeles from the Great Depression to the Present*. Berkeley: University of California Press, 2003.

Silka, Henry P., and Irene M. Almeida. *San Pedro: A Pictorial History*. San Pedro, CA: San Pedro Bay Historical Society, 1990.

Smith, Eugene W. *Trans-Atlantic Passenger Ships, Past and Present*. Boston: G.H. Dean, 1947.

Spenser, Jay P. *Whirlybirds: A History of the U.S. Helicopter Pioneers*. Seattle: University of Washington Press in Association with Museum of Flight, 1998.

Timmons, Todd. *Science and Technology in Nineteenth-Century America*. Westport, CT: Greenwood Press, 2005.

Wheelock, Walt. *Ferries of the South*. Glendale, CA: La Siesta Press, 1964.

Worden, William L. *Cargoes: Matson's First Century in the Pacific*. Honolulu: University Press of Hawaii, 1981.

JOURNALS AND MAGAZINES

Architectural Digest. "[Residence of Mr. and Mrs. O.R. Fuller, Los Feliz Hills, Los Angeles—Harry Hayden Whiteley, Architect]" (1930): 130–31.

Bail, Eli. "Long Beach Transit." *Motor Coach Age* (April–June 2004).

Bailey, Peter. "N.E.G.R.O. Charts New Path to Freedom." *Ebony* (April 1968): 49–56.

Bee-Hive (Pratt and Whitney). "The Quick and Nimble Carriers" (Fall 1957): 9.

Belinn, Clarence M. "Feeders Must Be Different." *Air Transport* (July 1945): 28–33.

Berry, M. "AM84-Los Angeles." *American Helicopter* (April 1948): 8–9.

Bourne, William D. "Cross Town Suburban Bus Lines." *Motor Coach Age* (January–March 2007).

Bus World. "Jitneys Return" (February 1980): 8.

Carey, Roland. "MV Vashon Island Was First Cross-Sound Ferry." *Marine Digest* (November 17, 1984): 11–14.

Crisis. "The Carswell Defeat: Racism Again Repulsed" (April 1970): 144–51.

Deverell, William F. "The Los Angeles 'Free Harbor Fight.'" *California History* (Spring 1991): 27.

Eckert, Ross D., and George W. Hilton. "The Jitneys." *The Journal of Law and Economics* 15, no. 2 (1972): 293.

Engineering News-Record. "Suspension Bridge Uses Welded Components" (April 11, 1963): 36–38.

Hindman, Jo. "The Big Ranch Fight." *Historical Society of Southern California Quarterly* 37, no 1 (March 1955): 57.

Hodgkins, Richard F. "Looking for a Place to Land." *Vertiflite* (May–June 1982): 18–21.

Hunter, Fred S. "Extra Section." *Airlift World Air Transportation* (June 1959): 58.

Kirsch, Jonathan. "The Persecution of Adriana Gianturco." *New West* (December 18, 1978): 54–60.

La Barbera, Joseph. "Joe Fawkes and the Aerial Swallow." *Westways* (February 1964): 26–27.

Motor Carrier. "Here's One on O.R." (November 1926): 12.

Myrick, David F. "The Determined Mrs. Rindge and Her Legendary Railroad." *Ventura County Historical Society Quarterly* 41, no. 3 n.d.: 9–35.

"New Meaning for 'Black Power'." *U.S. News & World Report* (July 22, 1968): 32–33.

Newsweek. "Watts, His Line" (January 1, 1968): 50–51.

Pacific Electric Magazine. "Building of Great Motor Transit System" (August 10, 1930): 5.

Pickering, E.H. "The First Helicopter Airline." *Flight* (December 1953): 26.

Plattner, C.M. "Peening Cited in Helicopter Crash," *Aviation Week & Space Technology* (January 13, 1969): 97.

Rafn, E.M. "The Fawkes and the Swallow." *Westways* (March 1976): 30–68.

"Rotary-Wing Progress and Problems." *Flying* (April 1963): 92.

Scavo, Jordan. "Water Politics and the San Fernando Valley: The Role of Water Rights in the 1915 Annexation and 1996–2002 Secession Campaigns." *Southern California Quarterly* 92, no. 2 (2010): 93–116.

Sikorsky, Igor L. "Promise of the Direct-Lift Airplane." *Aero Digest* (July 15, 1944): 74–75.

Spence, Clark C. "The Lancaster." *Pennsylvania History* (October 1958). http://journals.psu.edu/index.php/article/view/22626/22395.

Tabb, William K. "What Happened to Black Economic Development?" *Review of Black Political Economy* 9, no. 4 (1979): 392–415.

Taylor, Brian D. "Public Perceptions, Fiscal Realities, and Freeway Planning: The California Case." *Journal of the American Planning Association* 61, no. 1 (1995): 43–56.

Time. "Late for Dinner" (January 18, 1954): 63.

Wartenberg, Steve. "Airspur's New Commuter." *Vertiflite* (May–June 1983): 33–35.

Western Transit.

GOVERNMENT DOCUMENTS

Automated Guideway Transit: An Assessment of PRT and Other New Systems, including Supporting Panel Reports. Washington, D.C.: Government Printing Office, 1975.

Better Justifications Needed for Automated People Mover Demonstration Projects: Report to the Congress. Gaithersburg, MD: U.S. General Accounting Office, Document Handling and Information Services Facility, 1980.

Bullemer, R.J., C. Fratessa and John W. Billheimer. *The Santa Monica Freeway Diamond Lanes: Final Report*. Los Altos, CA: SYSTAN, 1977.

California Assembly. Concurrent Resolution No. 131, Statutes of California, 1961, 5,017.

California Department of Highways. *A Report on a Proposed Toll Highway Crossing of Los Angeles Harbor from San Pedro to Terminal Island*. Sacramento, CA, 1956.

California Department of Transportation. Local Agency Bridge List, 2012. http://www.dot.ca.gov/hq/LocalPrograms/hbrr99/2012-12-18-local-agency-bridge-list.xlsx.

California Governor's Commission on the Los Angeles Riots. *Violence in the City: An End or a Beginning?* Los Angeles, 1965.

California Public Utilities Commission. *Decisions of the Public Utilities Commission of the State of California.* San Francisco, CA, 1948– .

California Rail Passenger Development Plan: 1991 through 1996 Fiscal Years, as Required by Section 14036 of the Government Code. Sacramento, CA: Division of Rail, Caltrans, 1991.

California Railroad Commission. *Decisions of the Railroad Commission of the State of California.* San Francisco, CA, 1913–47.

City of Los Angeles Department of Transportation and Los Angeles Community Redevelopment Agency. *Preliminary Discussion of Possible Options for Use of the Bunker Hill Transit Tunnel.* 1990.

Los Angeles County Transportation Commission. *Los Angeles River and Tujunga Wash Channels: Conceptual Engineering Analysis of Potential Transportation Uses.* Los Angeles, 1991.

National Transportation Safety Board. *Aircraft Accident Report: Los Angeles Airways, Inc., S-61L Helicopter, N300Y, Compton, California, August 14, 1968.* Washington, D.C., 1969.

———. *Aircraft Accident Report: Los Angeles Airways, Inc., Sikorsky S-61L, N303Y, Paramount California, May 22, 1968.* Washington, D.C., 1969.

Southern California Commuter Rail Coordinating Council. *Southern California Commuter Rail 1991 Regional System Plan.* Los Angeles, 1991.

Southern California Rapid Transit District. Planning Department. *Analysis of Jitney Operations in Los Angeles.* Los Angeles, 1983.

Tomorrow's Transportation: New Systems for the Urban Future. Washington, D.C.: Government Printing Office, 1968.

Turnbull, Katherine F., and Sarah M. Hubbard. *7th National Conference on High-Occupancy Vehicle Systems: HOV Systems in a New Light: June 5–8, 1994, the Biltmore Hotel, Los Angeles, California.* Washington, D.C.: Transportation Research Board, National Research Council, 1995.

United States Army Corps of Engineers. *Los Angeles River Ecosystem Restoration Integrated Feasibility Report: Feasibility Study and Environmental Impact Statement/ Environmental Impact Report, Los Angeles County, California.* 2013. http://www.spl. usace.army.mil/Portals/17/docs/publicnotices/DraftIntegratedReport.pdf.

U.S. Department of Transportation, John A. Volpe National Transportation Systems Center. *Effects of Catastrophic Events on Transportation System Management and Operations Northridge Earthquake, January 17, 1994.* Cambridge, MA, 2002. http://ntl.bts.gov/lib/jpodocs/repts_te/13775_files/13775.pdf.

U.S. Department of Transportation, Office of the Secretary of Transportation. *Commuter and Express Bus Service in the SCAG Region: A Policy Analysis of Public and Private Operations.* Washington, D.C., 1983.

ARCHIVAL MATERIALS AND PAPERS

Adler, Patricia Rae. "Watts: From Suburb to Black Ghetto." PhD diss., University of Southern California, 1977.

Blue and White Bus Company Collection, Archives, Dorothy Peyton Gray Transportation Library.

Freeman, Dorothy Dobbins, Thelma Clark and Patricia Copley. *Pasadena Oral History Project: Interviews with Dorothy Dobbins Freeman.* Pasadena, CA: Pasadena Historical Society, 1982.

Gianturco, Adriana, and George F. Petershagen. *Oral History Interview with Adriana Gianturco: Director, California Department of Transportation, March 15, 1976–January 3, 1983, March 2–May 5, 1994, Sacramento, California.* 1994.

Los Angeles Board of Public Utilities and Transportation. *Annual Report.* Los Angeles City Records Center.

———. *Minutes.* Los Angeles City Records Center.

Peters, Arthur Gerald. "A History of the Helicopter Airline Industry." Master's thesis, California State University–San Francisco, 1973.

Records of U.S. District Court, Central District of California. Civil Dockets, Box 838, 17292-T. National Archives and Records Administration, Riverside, CA.

Special Committee on Air-Ocean Mail Contracts. Box 139, Record Group 46. National Archives and Records Administration, Washington, D.C.

Watts Record Collection. Los Angeles City Records Center.

Yeomans, Tim. "The Helicopter Air Service Passenger Program: A Retrospect." Graduate School of Management, University of California–Los Angeles, 1975.

NEWSPAPERS

California Eagle.
Daily Aztec (San Diego State University).
Daily Bruin (University of California–Los Angeles).
Daily Titan (California State University–Fullerton).
Fullerton Tribune.
Hollywood Citizen.
Huntington Park (CA) Daily Signal.
La Habra (CA) Daily Star Progress.
Le Temps (Paris, France).
Long Beach Independent.
Long Beach Press-Telegram.
Los Angeles Business Journal.
Los Angeles Daily News.
Los Angeles Downtown News.
Los Angeles Examiner.
Los Angeles Herald.
Los Angeles Herald-Examiner.
Los Angeles Sentinel.
Los Angeles Times.
Malibu Times.
New University (University of California–Irvine).
New York Times.
Oakland (CA) Tribune.
Ontario (CA) Daily Report.
Orange County Register.
Orange County Tribune.
Oxnard (CA) Daily Courier.
Pasadena Daily Star.
Pasadena Star News.
Pomona (CA) Inland Valley Daily Bulletin.
Pomona Progress Bulletin.
Riverside (CA) Press-Enterprise.
Sacramento Bee.
San Antonio (TX) Express.
San Gabriel Valley Daily Tribune.
San Pedro News Pilot.
Santa Ana Register.

Santa Monica Evening Outlook.
Santa Monica Outlook.
Simi Valley Enterprise.
Torrance (CA) Daily Breeze.
Torrance Herald.
Van Nuys News.
Wall Street Journal.
Washington Post.

COURT CASES

Fawkes v. City of Burbank, 188 Cal. 399 (March 14, 1922).
L.A. City Sch. Dist. v. Landier Inv. Co., 177 Cal. App. 2d 744 (February 9, 1960).
Los Angeles Airways, Inc. v. Hughes Tool Co., 156 Cal. Rptr. 805 (Court of Appeal of California, Second Appellate District, Division Four, July 16, 1979).
People v. Elliott, 115 Cal. App. 2d 410 (January 16, 1953).
Rindge Co. v. Los Angeles, 262 U.S. 700 (June 11, 1923).
Stearns v. Los Angeles City School District, 244 Cal. App. 2d 696 (September 8, 1966).
Succession of Landier, 25 So. 938 (May 1, 1899).

WEBSITES

The Arroyofest Project. Internet Archive, August 2003. https://web.archive.org/web/20120609015447/http://departments.oxy.edu/uepi/nela/publications/festReport.htm.
Arroyo Seco Foundation. "Arroyo Seco Foundation." http://www.arroyoseco.org/index.htm.
Friends of the LA River. "Friends of the L.A. River." http://www.folar.org.
Huntington Hospital. "A History of Huntington Hospital." http://www.huntingtonhospital.com/Main/HistoryofHuntington.aspx.
Island Express Helicopter Service. "Catalina Flights." http://www.islandexpress.com/flights.php.

LADOT Bicycle Services. "LADOT Bicycle Services—Bicycling in Los Angeles." http://www.bicyclela.org.

The Monorail Society. "The Monorail Society." http://www.monorails.org.

1964 New York World's Fair. "Attractions—Ford Motor Company—Page One." http://www.nywf64.com/ford01.shtml.

"90042" (blog). "Remembering The Great California Cycleway." December 14, 2010. http://highlandpark.wordpress.com/2010/12/14/remembering-the-great-california-cycleway.

Terminal Island. "Furusato: The Lost Village of Terminal Island." http://www.terminalisland.org/furusato.htm.

INDEX

S

T

ABOUT THE AUTHOR

Charles P. Hobbs's interest in public transportation began in 1984. While commuting on the bus, he started thinking about how public transportation could be improved. In 1989, he organized the archives of the Southern California Rapid Transit District Library (now known as the Dorothy Peyton Gray Transportation Library) as a student at UCLA's Graduate School of Library and Information Science. While doing so, he gained an interest in the history of public transportation in Southern California.

Author's collection.

In 1990, he joined the Southern California Transit Advocates (socata. net) and served as the group's newsletter editor between 1992 and 2005. In 2009, he started the "More than Red Cars" blog (morethanredcars.com), dedicated to the transportation history of Southern California.

He is a systems librarian at El Camino College Compton Center and an adjunct reference librarian at Irvine Valley College. A lifetime resident of Southern California, he currently resides in Fontana.

Visit us at
www.historypress.net
....
This title is also available as an e-book